CW00369845

Excel for Business Students

J Muir

Jim Muir is a Senior Lecturer in Business Computing at Bournemouth University. He has had a wide experience of teaching IT skills at a variety of levels.

DP Publications Ltd
Aldine Place
London W12 8AW
1993

A catalogue record for this book is available
from the British Library

Copyright J. Muir © 1993

ISBN 185805 029 4

Typeset by DP Publications Ltd

Printed by The Guernsey Press Company Ltd,
Braye Road, Vale, Guernsey, Channel Islands

Preface

Who should use this book

This book is aimed at students, on business and computing courses of all types, who need to learn how to use either Excel 3 or Excel 4. The learning material in this book requires minimal (or no) input from a lecturer and can be used as a self-instruction guide.

Computing skills are now more or less mandatory on all levels of business-related courses from BTEC National to degree, including courses in Finance, Tourism, Catering and Law, and many colleges are using Excel as their main vehicle to teach the use of spreadsheets.

Excel has rapidly been gaining ground on its main rival, Lotus 1-2-3, to become the industry-standard spreadsheet. It is available for both Apple and IBM personal computers (PCs). This book concentrates on Windows versions of Excel for IBM and compatible PCs.

Three levels and types of student are catered for:

Beginners learning Excel as part of an introduction to Business Computing, who need to perform simple but worthwhile tasks, e.g. creating simple spreadsheet models, amending them and displaying the results as graphs or charts.

Intermediate Students – as skills and confidence develop, students can perform more difficult tasks, e.g. using more complex functions and analysis tools, linking worksheets together and using tables.

Advanced Students – students studying the use of spreadsheets as a major course component will need to use the automated macro features of Excel and develop custom applications.

The material used in this book makes no assumptions about students' previous experience of either computing, business or financial accounting. Both the Excel skills and their business applications are explained in simple terms, and the author has deliberately avoided biasing the examples towards areas where specialised accountancy skills are required; the wider the range of potential uses the student is aware of the better.

Developments in Excel

Excel is produced by Microsoft Corporation, the US software company. It is specifically designed to operate using Windows, Microsoft's graphical operating environment.

Excel version 2 was introduced in 1987, version 3 in 1990, and the current version, Excel 4, in 1992.

Despite the continued popularity of Excel 2 and 3, especially in Education, many users have now changed to Excel 4. However, users of this book should not worry unduly about the different versions (and sub-versions such as 3.5) that exist. Microsoft has maintained upwards compatibility between versions. This means that for standard operations especially, the basic Excel menus, commands and screen layouts remain very similar in all versions. Additional features of later versions tend to appear as extra menu choices or 'buttons' on tool bars. Thus it is possible for this book to cover the most important features of versions 3 and 4. Excel 2 users also will find that nearly all of the activities in this book are achievable.

The scope of the book

There are already a large number of textbooks on the market covering Excel 3 or 4. Many are expensive, often US produced textbooks, offering comprehensive treatment, and aimed mainly at the advanced student or the industry practitioner. Of the few cheaper textbooks offered, none covers more than one version of Excel. This book covers the two latest versions.

A book of this size and price cannot be completely comprehensive, nor does it need to be. If computer literacy can be compared to learning a language, then one does not need to learn the complete contents of a dictionary to communicate effectively, one needs only the main vocabulary and grammar! Similarly the function of this book is to cover the essentials of Excel at elementary, intermediate and advanced level.

It will give students the confidence to perform the following essential tasks:

- ☐ Creating and using a spreadsheet
- ☐ Creating and using charts
- ☐ Using Excel database facilities
- ☐ Functions, tables and analysis tools.
- ☐ Building models and user applications
- ☐ Linking spreadsheets
- ☐ Macros and other automated features

All the activities in this book are based around business examples and have been tested by the author on BTEC and degree students. The Excel features that best solve typical business problems have been included. These features are introduced progressively by means of a series of student learning activities.

The Structure of the book

This book is divided into six chapters.

Chapters 1-3 cover elementary to intermediate Excel topics – spreadsheets, charts and databases.

Chapters 4 and 5 contain some further intermediate topics, e.g. linking spreadsheets, functions and cell protection, plus more advanced topics, e.g. macros, user applications, and analysis tools such as Solver and Scenario Manager. The extra features of later versions of Excel are mainly covered in chapters 4 and 5. Whenever it is important, the Excel version is clearly marked in the margin. Chapter 6 covers the use of macros to design a user application.

The active learning approach

The teaching/learning approach of this book departs from traditional textbook practice. Excel features are introduced in the context of practical business activities and problems to be solved, with the opportunity for further independent practice and consolidation.

Each chapter is divided into a number of short activities, which guide students step by step through the necessary skills. Chapters also contain consolidation activities – follow-up activities with minimal or no instructions that give students the chance to check their progress. Solutions are given at the end of the book, where appropriate. A summary of commands and functions is given at the end of each chapter.

Active learning is therefore encouraged, students have maximum support during initial learning and given opportunities for further reflection, theory and experimentation by independent activity. Students and/or lecturers will therefore be able to assess their progress.

A copyright-free $3\frac{1}{2}$" (720k) disk is available which includes the final version of the Excel files used in this book. This disk is available free to all lecturers who adopt the book as a course text.

Hints on active learning

Everyone learns at their own pace and in their own way; the following hints may be useful, whether you are learning independently or part of a lecturer-lead group.

❏ Do not omit or 'jump around' between activities; each activity builds upon knowledge and skills previously gained. You may also find that the Excel applications that you develop require earlier ones in order to work.

❏ Be patient and work slowly and methodically, especially in the early stages when progress may be very slow.

❏ Try not to compare your progress with others too much. Fastest is not always best!

☐ Don't try to achieve too much in one session. Time for rest and reflection is important.

☐ Remember that you are 'learning by doing'. Read the instructions carefully, study the effects your key strokes have on screen and ask yourself why.

☐ Mistakes are part of learning. No one can anticipate all the ones that you may make in this book. Again, consider the keys that you have pressed, and what is on the screen **before** making amendments; most mistakes are simple key press or typing errors.

☐ Make time to complete the independent learning exercises, especially if you are learning on your own. They are your best guide to your progress.

Introduction – Spreadsheets in Business

Since the microcomputer's initial impact on business in the 80's, three types of business software have emerged as industry standards, namely the word processor, the database management system and the spreadsheet. This is hardly surprising, as they fulfil three key business needs.

All businesses need to cope with the volumes of text that they create – letters, memos, reports etc. – hence the word processor.

They need to store and retrieve records of all types – stock, personnel, customer etc. – hence the need for database management systems.

Their third major need is to handle numeric data – sales, profits, financial forecasts, stock movements and mathematical models of all kinds. The spreadsheet meets this need.

For many years businesses have used manual spreadsheets – large sheets of squared paper divided into columns and rows. Managers have used these sheets of paper 'spread out' on their desks to analyse various types of business information. For example, it has been estimated that up to a third of a manager's time is typically spent preparing budgets. This involves such operations as manipulating, calculating and analysing numeric information, using formulae, inserting text and drawing graphs. When the data changes lengthy and tedious recalculation becomes necessary. A computer spreadsheet is simply the equivalent of this sheet of squared paper, with in-built calculating facilities.

A simple example of an Excel spreadsheet is shown below, calculating a student's personal finances; the columns represent the weeks and the rows various categories of income and expenditure. The balance at week end is carried forward to the next week using formulae.

You could use this data in a variety of ways:

- ☐ as a record of your past finances
- ☐ to budget for future expenditure
- ☐ to compare expenditure patterns month by month
- ☐ to experiment with the data to model possible increases in income or expenditure – what if rent rises by 10%?
- ☐ to draw graphs illustrating any of the above.

—	Microsoft Excel - Sheet1						

File Edit Formula Format Data Options Macro Window Help

Normal

D3

	A	B	C	D	E	F	G
1			PERSONAL FINANCES - TERM 1				
2	INCOME		Week 1				
3	Opening Bals.		0				
4	grant		500				
5	loan		400				
6	parents		300				
7	Total Income						
8							
9	EXPENDITURE						
10	accomodation		60				
11	food & Travel		30				
12	books		75				
13	other		20				
14	Total Expenditure						
15							
16	CLOSING BALS.						

Spreadsheet terminology

A spreadsheet is a grid of **vertical columns** and **horizontal rows**.

Where column and row intersect is a box or **cell**.

The cell **reference** or address consists of two co-ordinates – the column letter followed by the row number (as in a street map).

Cells can contain text (**labels**) or numbers (**values**).

Certain cells can also contain **formulae** which tell the spreadsheet to perform calculations, e.g. add a column or work out a percentage. These formulae ensure that totals are automatically recalculated when the values in the spreadsheet are changed.

Excel use the term 'worksheet' for their computer spreadsheet, I shall use it too from Chapter 1 onwards.

Advantages of spreadsheets

It is much easier to use a computerised spreadsheet, such as Excel, than to perform manual calculations. A spreadsheet is a general-purpose tool that can be used to solve a wide variety of problems – any information that can be represented as columns and rows.

The advantages of spreadsheets should now be obvious:

❑ Reducing the drudgery of calculations
❑ Reducing errors
❑ Freeing user time to concentrate on problem solving
❑ Allowing users to examine alternative solutions
❑ Producing quicker results

In the chapters that follow you will realise these advantages for yourself and gain an important business skill.

Contents

Chapter 1: Creating and Using a Worksheet

Introduction to the Chapter

In this chapter you'll learn such essential preliminaries as starting up the Excel package, using the mouse, and finding your way around the worksheet screen.

Then you'll create your first worksheet and find out how to input and alter data. With a little practice, you will find the next stages straightforward – using formulae to perform the calculations.

Finally we'll learn how to save and print the worksheet.

Make sure that you read and follow the instructions in these activities carefully. You are bound to make a few mistakes – these are part of learning – but you will learn how to put them right for yourself.

Summary of Skills Covered

Key:

Skill	Activity	Skill	Activity
Addition	4.1	Formulae	4
Absolute addressing	15.7	Freezing titles and labels	8.9
Averages, calculating	15	Gridlines, removing	8.8
Bold text, adding	8.1	Help, using	2.12
Cell borders, adding	8.7	Loading Excel	1
Cell data		Menus, using	2.10
alignment	8.3	Mouse operation	2.6
clearing	4.4	Number formats, selecting	8.4
copying, cutting and pasting	7	New worksheet, creating	15
editing	3.3	Percentages, calculating	15
entering	3	Printing a worksheet	9
Cell selection	2.9	Relative addressing	15.7
Centring Titles	8.6	Retrieving a worksheet	6
Character size	8.2	Rows	
Columns		deleting	8.5
widening	3.4	enlarging	3.5
deleting and Inserting	8.5	Screen size, changing	2.5
Copying a worksheet	11.3	Saving the worksheet	5
Deleting a worksheet	14	Scrolling	2.7
Dialogue Boxes, using	2.10	Subtraction	4.6
Drive, changing	6.4	Shortcut keys	2.11
Exiting Excel	2.13	SUM command	4.1
Fonts, selecting	8.2	Templates, making	13
Formatting the worksheet	8,16	Text, adding blocks	8.10 & 15.10

Activity 1. Loading and Running Excel

Excel is a Windows application. This means that Excel will not run unless the Microsoft Windows software package is already loaded – up and running.
How this is done will depend on how your computer has been set up. The following instructions will cover most situations.

1.   First turn on your computer (and the screen too if necessary). If a screen dispaly appears that resembles Figure 1.1 below then Windows has automatically loaded. Proceed to section 4 now.

2.   If Windows has not loaded then try the following:
     Some PCs, especially those in colleges, display a main menu system when first turned on. Is there a menu option for Windows or Excel? If so take it, i.e. type the option number followed by the Enter or Return key.
     This large L-shaped key on the right of the keyboard is marked with a curled arrow.
     Perhaps all that displays is the prompt C:\> or similar. This is the DOS or operating system prompt.
     Type WIN and press the Enter Key.
     If this doesn't work try the following:
     Type the command DIR/W and press the Enter Key.
     A list of names appear in square brackets; these are names of directories.
     Identify one named [WINDOWS] or similar.
     Type the command CD\WINDOWS and press the Enter key. You are now in the directory (part of the hard disk) that contains the Windows programs.
     Type the command WIN and press the Enter key.
     Windows should now load – see Figure 1.1 below.

3.   Look at Figure 1.1 carefully (your Windows startup screen may look slightly different, depending on what programs you have on your PC and how Windows was installed)
     One window is open at the moment, the Program Manager. In the window are various icons – small pictures of applications – that can be run from Windows. If you can already see one entitled 'Microsoft Excel' or 'Microsoft Excel 4.0' then skip to section 6.

4.   Use your desktop mouse to move the arrow-shaped pointer on screen; this is called the screen pointer or cursor. It will change shape, depending on the operation that you are carrying out.
     Move it on top of the Windows Applications icon.
     Now click the mouse button twice in quick succession – if there is more than one button on your mouse then use the leftmost button.

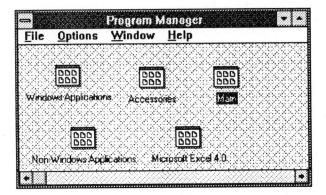

Figure 1.1

5. A further window appears, titled 'Windows Applications' – see Figure 1.2. Again, the number of icons in this window will depend on how your PC has been set up, and the version of Excel that you are using.

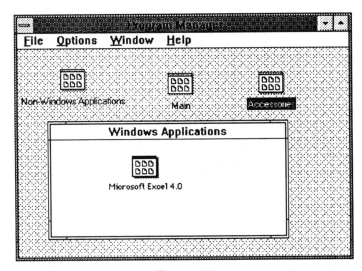

Figure 1.2

6. Identify the Microsoft Excel icon, move the screen pointer on top of it, and 'double click' as before.
   If a further window opens, revealing another Excel icon, then double click this too.
   Excel will begin to load from the PC's hard disk (confirmed by an hour-glass symbol) and after a few seconds a blank worksheet screen appears.

Activity 2. The Worksheet Screen – Mouse, Commands and Menus.

1. Let's do a quick tour of the worksheet screen.
    Remember that, as we said in the Preface, a spreadsheet or worksheet is
    the equivalent of a large sheet of paper, divided into columns and rows.

2. Keep referring to the labelled diagram below; don't worry if your screen is
    slightly different, we're just identifying the main features at the moment.

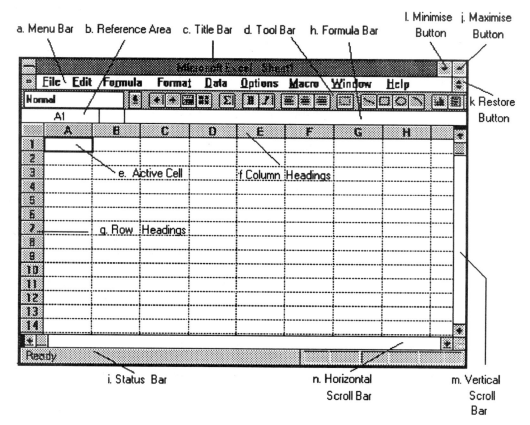

Figure 1.3

3. a. **The Menu Bar.** The menu bar at the top of the screen shows a list of
        menu options – File, Edit, Formula etc.
        The Excel commands are grouped under these menus.

    b. **The Reference Area.** Shows the row and column number of the active
        cell – see e below.

    c. **The Title Bar.** Whenever a new worksheet is opened Excel gives it a
        temporary or default name, Sheet1, Sheet2 etc. This name will change
        when you save the worksheet.

d. **The Tool Bar.** (Excel versions 3 and 4 only).
    The tool bar is immediately below the menu bar; it consists of a row of buttons that you 'click' to carry out some of the commonest Excel tasks – drawing a chart, adding a column etc. They are in effect shortcut versions of the menu commands. In this book we concentrate mainly on the menu versions of commands, but will be introducing useful tools as the need arises.
    A key to the tool bars is included at the end of this chapter.

e. **The Active Cell.** At the moment the top left cell A1 is the active cell – shown by a heavy border. As we will see, you cannot enter information into a cell unless it has first been selected and made 'active'.

f. **Column Headings** and   These contain the column references (letters)
                                                      and the row references (numbers). Jointly
g. **The Row headings.**   they give the cell reference.

h. **The Formula Bar.** Shows the formula or data entered in the active cell. This is a new worksheet so all the cells are blank.

i. **The Status Bar.** Displays information about the current command; no command has been issued yet so it reads 'Ready'.
    At the top right of the screen are various buttons marked with arrow heads; these control the size of the worksheet screen:

j. **The Maximise Button.** Increases the window to full-screen size. There are two – one for the whole window and one for the cell area.

k. **The Restore Button.** Restores the window size.

l. **The Minimise Button.** Reduces the screen to a small icon.

m. and n. **The Vertical and Horizontal Scroll Bars.** Allow you to move around the worksheet.

The present worksheet window can only show a small fraction of the total worksheet size; potentially a worksheet can be 256 columns across and 16,384 rows down!

4. Now that we've identified the basic screen components let's try some of them out; keep referring to Figure 1.3. First we will experiment with the screen size; this often causes problems when you're starting out.

5. **Screen Size.** Move the screen pointer onto the Minimise button at the top right of the screen. Click the mouse button once. The worksheet disappears, and you return to the Windows screen.

    At the bottom left of the screen is a second Excel icon; this represents the minimised worksheet.

    Move the screen pointer onto this and 'double click', i.e. click the mouse button twice in quick succession.

    The worksheet Sheet1 reappears – try again if it doesn't. Now click the Maximise button once. The worksheet enlarges to display more cells.

    Click the Restore button and the worksheet reverts to its previous size.

    It is also possible to alter the size of the worksheet window by 'dragging' the sides.

    Move the pointer to the bottom right-hand edge of the worksheet – the screen pointer changes to a double-headed arrow when correctly located.

    Now press down the mouse button **and keep it pressed down.**

    Drag the edge of the worksheet diagonally towards the top left of the screen until you have reached cell D8. Then let go.

    Your worksheet window should now look like Figure 1.4.

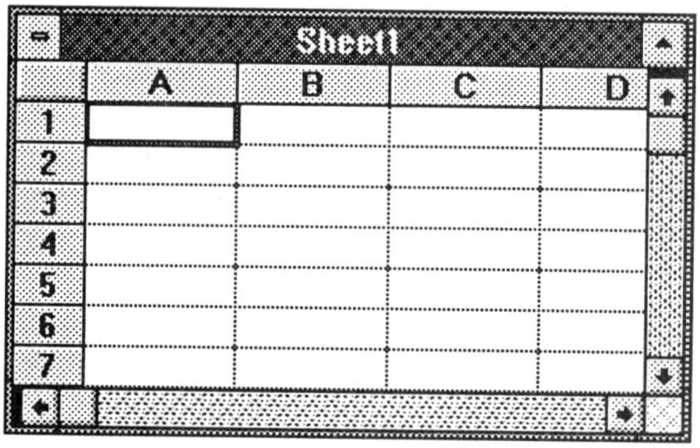

Figure 1.4

Restore the worksheet window to full size by reversing this dragging process.

6. **Mouse Control.** You have now learnt the 3 basic mouse actions:

    clicking – locate screen pointer, press mouse button once

    double clicking – locate screen pointer and press mouse button twice in quick succession

    dragging – locate screen pointer, hold down button while moving mouse, release button.

    From now on I shall be using these names to refer to these actions.

7. **Scrolling Around the Screen.** There are several ways to change the part of the worksheet window currently being displayed on screen. Try these:
    Move your pointer to the vertical scroll bar and locate it on the down arrow button. Click once and the worksheet scrolls up a few rows – notice the row references change.
    Hold the button down and the rows scroll continuously. Now use the up arrow button to reverse the scrolling. Row 1 will eventually move to the top of the window again.
    Now move the pointer halfway down the scroll bar and click. The rows scroll down, a screenful at a time.
    Now identify the square scroll box on the scroll bar.
    Try dragging this box – it will scroll the worksheet more quickly.
    Repeat these operations for the horizontal scroll bar which controls the columns.

8. **Keyboard Commands.** Let's try out some keyboard commands which also change the screen position:
    Hold down the Ctrl key and press the Home key – you are returned to the top of the worksheet – cell A1.
    Hold down the Ctrl key and press the down arrow key on the keyboard – you are taken to the last row of the worksheet. (if the worksheet is not empty you are moved to the last row containing an entry)
    Now hold down the Ctrl key and press the right arrow key. You are taken to the last column of the worksheet.
    Now try out the key combinations,
    >   Ctrl – left arrow
    >   Ctrl – up arrow
    You will return to the top of the worksheet again.
    (The Page Up and Page down keys can also be used)

    Hint. These keys are vital – not only in moving to cells, but also in finding your way back to the correct part of the worksheet – you can avoid that lost panicky feeling when all your data seems to have disappeared!

9. **Selecting Cells.** Return to the top of the worksheet and click cell A2. You have just selected a cell, the reference box shows that it has become the active cell.
    Now move the screen pointer to cell C3, using either the mouse or the arrow keys on the keyboard.
    This becomes the active cell.
    Experiment a few more times and select cells H12, F18 and E14 in the current window.
    Now using the screen controls, select cells M84, HJ127 and E216 in turn.
    One can also select groups or ranges of cells and whole columns or rows.
    Move to cell A1 and drag the screen pointer down and across to cell D6. Release the mouse button and 24 cells should be selected in all – see Figure 1.5

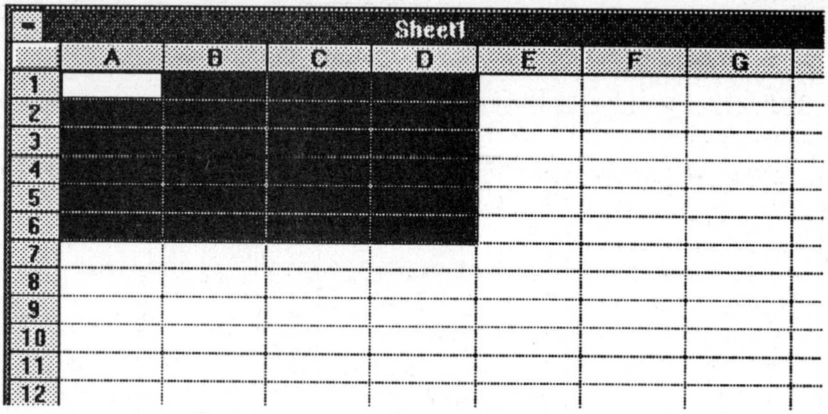

Figure 1.5

Notice that A1, the first cell selected, remains white while the others go dark. A1 remains the active cell in the range.

The cell range A1 to D6 is now selected.

Deselect this cell range by clicking the worksheet outside the selected range of cells.

Hint. Selecting or 'highlighting' cells is an essential first step in many operations; it requires a little practice to select groups of cells accurately.

10. **Menus and Dialogue Boxes.** To complete the tour of the Excel screen we'll select some commands from the Menu Bar.

    Menus are your major means of issuing commands. Choosing a command involves two steps, opening the menu and selecting an option.

    Move the screen pointer onto the Menu Bar and click the word Formula. This opens the Formula menu and displays a pull-down menu of commands.

    Click elsewhere on the worksheet and close the Formula menu.

    Now open the Formula menu again; this time click the Goto option.

    A dialogue box appears – see Figure 1.6.

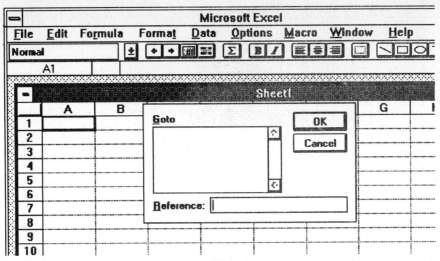

Figure 1.6

Dialogue boxes are used when you need to enter some further information about the option that you have chosen.

Note that a message in the Status Bar tells you to press the F1 key for further help.

Do this and a help screen appears explaining the Goto command.

Use the scroll bars on the Help screen to read the information about the Goto command.

Return to the dialogue box as follows:

Move the screen pointer to the Menu Bar **at the top of the Help window.**

Click the Exit option – you are returned to the Goto dialogue box.

Enter C4 in the Reference box and then click the OK button. The Goto option goes to the named cell (C4) and activates it.

11. **Shortcut Keys.** Some Excel users may prefer to issue commands from the keyboard, rather than using the mouse and pull-down menus. You will notice that each menu title on the Menu Bar has one of its letters underlined – File, Edit, Formula etc.

    If you hold down the Alt key then type the appropriate letter the menu selection will be displayed – try this.

    Press the Alt or the F10 key to close the menu. There are similar shortcuts for the menu selections themselves, and many other Excel features.

    In this book we shall use the mouse rather than the keyboard to issue commands.

12. **Using Help.** Excel provides a comprehensive online help and tutorial facility on basic operations, concepts and commands. You can call Help either by pressing the F1 key, or by using the Help menu on the menu bar.

    Excel Help is also context sensitive – you can get specific guidance on what you are doing currently, as you discovered in section 10.

Excel 3   **Excel 3.** Open the Help menu and select the Index option. This opens a further help screen – see Figure 1.7

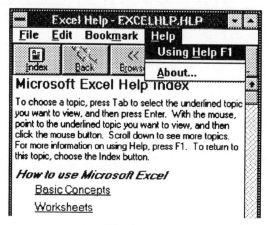

Figure 1.7

Now move the pointer to the Menu Bar **on the help screen.**
Open the Help menu and select the command
'Using Help F1'.
Scroll through the information on this screen. It will tell you how to use Excel's comprehensive help system.
Exit help by opening the File menu on the help screen and selecting the Exit option. You are returned to the worksheet.

Excel 4   **Excel 4 – Help Menu.** Open the Help menu and select the Contents option. Now move the pointer to the Menu Bar **on the help screen** and open the Help menu.
Select the option 'How to Use Help'.
Scroll through the information on this screen. It will tell you how to use Excel's comprehensive help system.
Exit Help by opening the File menu on the help screen and selecting the Exit option. You are returned to the worksheet.

Excel 4   **Excel 4 – Help Button.** Look at the Tool Bar at the top of the screen. The Help button is marked with a question mark and arrow – see the key to the Tool Bar at the end of this chapter.
Click the Help button once; the screen pointer changes to a question mark.
Open the Formula menu and select the Goto option. Excel offers you help on this option.
Exit from Help as before.

13. **Exiting from Excel.** Move the screen pointer onto the File option on the Menu Bar and click.

The File menu opens. Click the Exit option.
You leave Excel. As you have entered no data in the worksheet you are not prompted to save it.

Activity 3. Entering Data into the Worksheet

Now that we know our way around the worksheet screen we can create our first worksheet. We'll choose a simple example – managing one's personal finances.
Look at Figure 1.8:

	A	B	C	D	E	F	G
1			PERSONAL FINANCES - TERM 1				
2	INCOME		Week 1				
3	Opening Bals.		0				
4	grant		500				
5	loan		400				
6	parents		300				
7	Total Income						
8							
9	EXPENDITURE						
10	accomodation		60				
11	food & Travel		30				
12	books		75				
13	other		20				
14	Total Expenditure						
15							
16	CLOSING BALS.						

Figure 1.8

The worksheet is based around a student's income and expenditure for a term. Later on you can adapt it if you like to suit your own circumstances; for the moment enter the data exactly as shown here.

1. First enlarge the worksheet window if necessary by clicking the Maximise button on the worksheet. (see Activity 2, Section 3)

2. **Entering Titles and Labels.** First click cell C1 to activate it. The reference C1 is now displayed in the reference area and the cell is outlined with a border.

Now enter the title shown in Figure 1.8. – PERSONAL FINANCES – TERM 1' – use capital letters. Notice that the title displays in the Formula Bar as you type it.

Press Enter and the title appears, displayed across several cells; this is as it should be.

We are now ready to enter the cell labels in column A. (A label is anything like a column or row heading that labels or identifies cells)

Activate cell A2 (i.e. click it) and enter the first label INCOME.

Whenever you enter or change a cell's contents you need to complete the entry. There are several ways to do this:

- ❏ press Enter
- ❏ click the next cell
- ❏ press one of the arrow keys on the keyboard
- ❏ click the 'tick' box that appears next to the Formula Bar

Hint. Forgetting to complete the entry causes a number of problems, e.g. menu options being dimmed and unavailable. Always check this if your next command fails to execute.

Text is automatically aligned to the left of the cell. Carry on and complete all the labels in column 1. Don't worry if some labels overlap into the next column.

Use the Backspace key to correct any errors that you notice while completing an entry.

Don't worry about errors that you notice at a later stage – we will correct them in section 3 of this activity.

Complete the column heading for week 1.

3. **Editing Cell Contents.** Notice that the label 'Accommodation' has been misspelt with only one 'm'.

First click the cell to activate it. The text appears in the Formula Bar at the top of the screen.

Now move the screen pointer onto the text 'Accomodation' **in the Formula Bar** – the pointer changes to a vertical bar.

Position the pointer in front of the 'm' and click to place the insertion point.

Type the extra 'm' and press Enter.

The cell is amended

Hint. You cannot edit cell contents directly, but only via the Formula Bar.

Deleting. If you need to delete any character, you must do so via the Formula Bar in the same way as above:

- ❏ Use the Delete key to delete to the right of the insertion point
- ❏ Use the Backspace key to delete to the left of the insertion point.
- ❏ Relocate the pointer by clicking another cell.

Now alter the text in cell A5 to 'Bank loan'.

Overtyping. To overtype the contents of a cell, just select the cell and start typing. All the cell contents will be overwritten.
There is no need to delete the contents first.

4. **Widening Columns.** Some of the labels in Column A are too wide for their cells. Try out these alternative methods:

   a. Locate the screen pointer on the vertical line that separates column designator A from column designator B.
       The pointer changes to a double-headed arrow.
       Now press down the mouse button and drag the column to the right until its width is 16.00. The width is given in the reference area.

   b. Click the column designator, i.e. the 'A' in the column heading. The whole column is selected.
       Open the Format menu and select Column Width.
       A dialogue box is displayed.
       Enter the new width as 16.00, and click the OK button or,

   c. click the Best Fit button to adjust the column to the width of the longest entry.

5. **Altering the Row Height.** We will now make row 1 higher to emphasise the title.
   Locate the screen pointer on the horizontal line that separates row designator 1 from row designator 2.
   Drag the row height to 15.00.
   (You can also use the option Row Height on the Format menu to achieve the same result.)

6. **Entering Numeric Data.** This is the same procedure as for cell labels.
   Activate cell C3 and type 0.

   Hint. Make sure that this is the number 0 and not the letter O (a common source of error).

   Press Enter and the number is aligned to the right of the cell.
   Complete the other income and expenditure items as shown in Figure 1.8;
   Use the down arrow key to complete each entry.
   To amend the data use the same procedures as in section 3.

   Hint. If the number entered is too wide for the column Excel alerts you to this by a row of hash signs (####). You must then widen the column.

Activity 4. Using Formulae

Formulae are used as to perform a variety of operations, such as calculations.
A formula is placed in a cell like text or numbers. It can be very simple, such as adding the contents of 2 cells, or complex, containing mathematical or financial functions.
You must always start a formula with an equal sign; it tells Excel that you are about to apply a formula to a cell.

1. **Addition.** Now that we have entered the first week's income and expenditure figures we can add them using formulae.
   To calculate total income, first activate cell C7 and type an = sign. The = sign appears in the formula bar, alongside two buttons, a 'tick' and a 'cross' button.
   Now type the formula SUM(C3:C6) This is the formula to add or sum the range of four cells C3 to C6.
   Click the tick button next to the formula (or press Enter)
   The results of the formula are displayed in cell C7 – the income total of 1200.
   If you make a mistake entering the formula or get an error message, refer to Activity 3, Section 3.
   SUM is an Excel function or built-in formula, and is a lot quicker than typing the full formula C3+C4+C5+C6.
   Functions and formulae may be typed in upper or lower case.
   SUM is also expandable – if another row is inserted into this range of 4 cells at a later stage, say between rows 4 and 5, by using SUM the new cell would automatically be included in the range.
   This is not the case if one types the formula out in full using the + sign.

2. **Adding Up Columns – Shortcuts.** We will now use a formula to add up the total expenditure.
   Activate cell C14 and type =SUM(
   Move the screen pointer to the first expenditure item, cell C10.
   Hold down the mouse button and drag the pointer down to cell C13.
   Four cells are enclosed by a dotted box.
   Type the final right bracket) and the formula bar should read SUM(C10:C13)
   (If you have made a mistake then click the cross (X) box on the formula bar and start again.)
   Click the tick box and the result of the formula – 185 – is displayed.

3. **Amending Formulae – Error Messages.** If you make a mistake with a formula then the basic procedure is the same as amending text or numbers – see Activity 3, Section 3.

Try the following:

Activate cell C7 and move the pointer onto the formula bar.

Alter the formula to SUM(C3:C7) and click the tick box to execute the new formula.

The error message 'Cannot resolve circular references' appears and help is offered at the bottom of the screen. Click the OK button in the dialogue box.

As C7 is the 'destination' cell – the cell containing the formula – it cannot also be one of the cells to be summed as this is 'circular'.

Correct the formula to its original SUM(C3:C6) and execute it again.

Excel has a range of error messages, we'll look at one more for the moment.

Activate cell C14 and amend SUM to SIM.

When you execute this formula (use the Enter key or tick box) the error message #NAME? appears in the cell.

Don't correct it just yet.

4. **Clearing Cell Contents.** Move the screen pointer to the Menu Bar at the top of the screen.

   Click the Edit menu to select it.

   The Edit menu opens – select the option Clear.

   When the dialogue box appears click the OK button – the cell is cleared.

5. **Adding Columns – the SUM Button.** We need to add the expenditure cells again.

   Activate cell C14 if necessary.

   The Sum button is on the tool bar and is marked with the Greek letter Sigma (like a capital M on its side)

   Click the Sum button once and the formula appears in the formula bar. Check that it is correct.

   Click the sum button again and the formula is executed, the total 185 appears in cell C14.

6. **Subtraction Formulae.** We now need to subtract total expenditure from total income to find the closing balance for week 1.

   Activate cell C16 and type the formula =C7-C14

   Execute the formula as before and the closing balance for week 1 (1015) appears in cell C16.

   Your worksheet should now be the same as Figure 1.9.

	A	B	C	D	E	F	G	H
1			PERSONAL FINANCES - TERM 1					
2	INCOME		Week 1					
3	Opening Bals.		0					
4	grant		500					
5	loan		400					
6	parents		300					
7	Total Income		1200					
8								
9	EXPENDITURE							
10	accomodation		60					
11	food & Travel		30					
12	books		75					
13	other		20					
14	Total Expenditure		185					
15								
16	CLOSING BALS.		1015					
17								
18								
19								
20								

Cell reference: C16 = C7-C14

Figure 1.9

Activity 5. Saving Your Worksheet.

Note: At the moment your worksheet is only saved in the computer's main memory. It could be lost for ever if your PC crashes or the power goes off. You need to save it permanently as a named file on disk.

In this book I make the assumption that you will want to save your work on a floppy disk or diskette (A drive) not on the computer's hard disk (C drive).

All future references assume this.

1. Open the File menu (click File on the Menu Bar) and select the Save option. A dialogue box appears – see Figure 1.10.
    It will vary slightly, depending on the version of Excel that you are using.

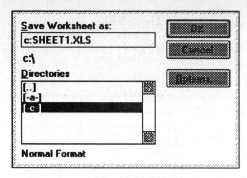

Figure 1.10

2. At the moment the worksheet has the default name SHEET1.XLS.
   .XLS is the extension automatically assigned to all Excel worksheet files, but we want to save it under a more meaningful name than Sheet1.
   A filename can be 1 – 8 characters long, and can consist of any combination of letters, numbers and certain special characters ('!?__ etc.) but not blanks or dashes.
   First make sure that you have a suitable, formatted floppy disk in the diskette drive.
   Type the file name A:\TERM1
   If you have made a mistake click the Cancel button and start again, otherwise click the OK button.
   The file takes a few seconds to save to A drive – the drive light should come on to confirm this.

3. When you return to your worksheet you will see the name of the worksheet displayed in the title bar.

   Hint. Get into the habit of saving your document regularly as you work, not just when you exit Excel. Remember that any data keyed in since your last Save command has not yet been saved permanently.

   This feature can be useful if you have made some irrecoverable error in your worksheet; you can close the worksheet without saving the errors, then open it again.
   The worksheet will be retrieved as it was before your last Save command.

4. At this point use the File menu to exit from Excel.

Activity 6. Loading an Existing Worksheet

Your worksheet TERM1 has been saved to disk on A drive as an Excel file. To work on it again you must use this name to retrieve it from disk and load it into main memory.

1. Start Excel again. A new blank worksheet appears with the default name SHEET1. We will close it as we want to work on an existing worksheet.
   Open the File menu and select the Close option (not Exit).
   The Excel screen goes blank, as no worksheet is in use.

2. If you saved your TERM1 worksheet to a diskette then obviously the first step is to ensure that this disk is in drive A!
   Open the File menu and select Open. A dialogue box appears.
   It is similar to Figure 1.10 in the last activity.

3. **Retrieving a File by Typing the Name.** If you are sure of the file name and the drive (as we should be) then simply type them in the File Name box – it is already selected.
   Type A:\TERM1.XLS and Click the OK button.
   The file will load from disk and appear on screen. If not check your spelling and that you are using the correct diskette.
   Open the File menu and select the Close option again.

4. **Retrieving a File From the File List.** Alternatively you can open a file by choosing it from a list.
   Open the File menu and select the Open option.
   This time we may need to select the drive.

Excel 3   **Excel 3.** Find the [-a-] symbol in the Directories box – you may need to use the scroll bar to bring it into view.
   Click the [-a-] symbol, then click the OK button.

Excel 4   **Excel 4.** Move the screen pointer onto the Drives box and click the Down Arrow symbol. Select the a: drive icon.
   The worksheet TERM.XLS appears in the File Name box to the left.
   Click it to select it, then click the OK button again.
   The file will load from disk and appear on screen.

Activity 7. Copying Cells and Deleting Data

At the moment we only have data for week 1. We are going to copy this data into the next column to create week 2, and modify certain cells. We will then experiment with a number of ways to move, copy, and delete cells. They are all useful in certain contexts, so make sure that you try out all these activities.

1. **Copying and Pasting.** This involves selecting one or more cells, and then copying them to another part of the worksheet.
   First select the Week 1 data; move the screen pointer onto cell C2, and drag down to column C16.
   Open the Edit menu and select Copy (not Cut)
   The selected area is now enclosed by a flowing dotted line called the Marquee.
   (Whenever you copy cells, Excel stores them in a temporary memory area called the Clipboard. They stay there until they are replaced by some other Copy command)

Excel 4   **Excel 4 Users** may use the Copy tool on the Toolbar – see the Toolbar key at the end of this chapter – instead of the Edit Copy command.

   The next stage of the process is to indicate where the cells are to be copied to.
   Activate cell D2 – the cell where you want to start pasting from.
   Open the Edit menu and select Paste.
   The cells are copied to a new location, and the Marquee remains around the area that you copied, allowing you to paste it again if you wish.
   The Marquee may now be removed by pressing the Esc key.
   If you have made a mistake then open the Edit menu and select the Undo Paste command.
   Notice that not only the data but also the formulae are copied. Excel automatically adjusts the cell references in the formulae to refer to their new location in Column D. Click the formulae cells in column D to check this.
   Now amend the heading of the copied cells to 'WEEK 2'.

2. **Cutting and Pasting.** Cutting cells physically removes them from their original location so that they can be pasted to a new one. It is similar operation to copying.
   Select the cells for week 2, i.e. cell range D2 to D16.
   Open the Edit menu and select the Cut option; the cells are surrounded by the marquee as before.
   Activate cell E2, then open the File menu and select Paste.
   This time the week 2 columns are moved a column to the right, leaving column D blank.

3. Let's now clear the week 2 column – in our next activity we will learn a quicker way of copying columns using the Fill Right command.
   Select the cells in column E if necessary, then open the Edit menu and select Clear. A dialogue box appears.
   Click the OK button and the cells are permanently cleared – the contents are deleted; no copy is made to the clipboard as with the Cut and Copy commands.
   As before you can use the Undo command to restore deleted data

4. **Copying Cells Using Fill Right.** Move the screen pointer onto cell C2. Hold down the mouse button and drag down the column to cell C16.
   Keeping the mouse button pressed down, drag the screen pointer across to select the same number of cells in the next column. Now let go.
   You should now have selected 2 columns – see Figure 1.11.

	A	B	C	D
1			PERSONAL FINANCE	
2	INCOME		week1	
3	Opening Bals.		0	
4	grant		500	
5	loan		400	
6	parents		300	
7	total income		1200	
8				
9	EXPENDITURE			
10	accommodation		60	
11	food & travel		30	
12	books		75	
13	other		20	
14	Total Expenditure		185	
15				
16	Closing Bals		1015	

Figure 1.11

You may need to try more than once to get it right.

5. Now open the Edit menu and select Fill Right.
   The contents of column C – data and formulae – are copied to column D.
   If the copying is incorrect then open the Edit menu again and select Undo Fill Right.
   Select cell D2 and amend the column label to 'Week 2'.

6. The values in cells D4 to D6 will need to be deleted; they are 'one-off' income items only applying to week 1. Drag from D4 down to D6 to select these 3 cells.
   Open the Edit menu and select Clear.
   Click the OK button in the dialogue box.
   Notice how the totals in column D are automatically recalculated.

If you have cleared the wrong cells then open the Edit menu again and select Undo Clear.

Notice that your closing balance for week 2 is now a negative amount, an insolvent -185.

However this is because we have not yet carried forward the closing balance of 1015 from week 1 to the opening balance for week 2. Let's do this with a formula.

7. Activate cell D3 and type =C16
   We want the value in cell D5, the opening balance for week 2, to equal C16, the closing balance for week 1.
   Click the Tick button to execute the formula and the week 2 totals are recalculated – your closing balance for week 2 is now a healthy 830.

8. Now make the following amendments to week 2:

Food and travel	35
Books	15

   Make the amendments by activating the cells, keying in the new values, and pressing Enter or clicking the Tick button. There is no need to clear the cells first.

9. We can now use week 2 as our model for the next 3 weeks.
   First select the week 2 values and the 3 adjacent columns, i.e. 4 columns in all, cells D2 – G16.
   Then use the Fill Right command as before.
   The contents of column D (week 2) are copied into columns E,F and G.
   Amend the week numbers for columns E to G.

   Hint. Remember to use the Undo command, as before if you make a mistake.

   The closing balance at the end of week 5 should be 495. Remember to save the changes that you have made.

Activity 8. Formatting the Worksheet

You now have a valid working model of the first 5 weeks finances for Term 1. However its final appearance can be improved considerably.
Excel allows you to alter the worksheet format in many ways, including the type size and style, and column width and alignment.

1. **Emboldening.** First we will put the title and cell labels in bold.
   Drag to select the title and the column headings – cells A1 to G2.
   Click the Bold button on the tool bar – marked with a capital B. The cells are emboldened.
   You may also wish to use the Italic button, marked with a capital I.
   You can also embolden using the Format menu.
   Select the row labels in column 1.

   Excel 3 **Excel 3.** Open the Format Menu and select the Font option.
   A dialogue box appears; find the sub-box entitled Style, and click the Bold button – a cross appears indicated that this option is selected.

   Excel 4 **Excel 4.** Open the Format Menu and select the Font option.
   A dialogue box appears; find the sub-box entitled Font Style, and click the Bold option.Click the OK button, the titles and labels are now in bold.
   Repeat this operation to embolden the closing balances in row 16.

2. **Character Size and Fonts.** Select the row labels in column A.
   Open the Format menu and select Font.
   Identify the sub-box called Size from the dialogue box. At the moment all characters on the worksheet are the default size of 10 point.
   Click 8 – you may need to scroll it into view.
   You may also like to experiment with different fonts or typefaces, which are shown in the Font box. The ones that your current printer is capable of printing are shown in black rather than pale grey.
   Now click the OK button – the cell labels are now in a smaller type, and any font changes are also shown.

   Excel 4 **Excel 4 only. The Increase/Decrease Font Size Buttons.** Select the Cell containing the worksheet title – PERSONAL FINANCES – TERM 1.
   Click the Increase Font Size Button – it is marked with a large A symbol – see the Toolbar key at the end of the chapter.
   The font size increases and the row also increases in height to accommodate it. You can keep doing this until the maximum height is reached.
   Now use the Decrease Font size button to reduce the title to a more suitable height.

3. **Alignment.** At the moment the numeric values are aligned to the right of the cells. This is the default for numbers, however it can look neater to centre them under the column headings.

   Select all the numeric data for week 1, i.e. cells C3 to C16.

   Open the Format menu and choose Alignment.

   Now click the 'Center' button on the dialogue box, followed by the OK button. The cells are aligned centrally.

   Alignment Buttons. Let's repeat this operation for weeks 2 – 5. First select this cell range. On the tool bar are a group of 3 alignment buttons, showing left, centre and right alignment – see Figure 1.12

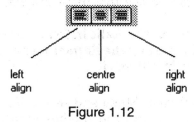

   left   centre   right
   align   align   align

   Figure 1.12

   Click the centre button. The value are centred.

4. **Number and Currency Formats.** Let's alter the way numeric values are displayed. First select all the numeric cells (C3 – G16).

   Open the Format menu and select the Number option. Select the 0.00 option from the list displayed, then click the OK button. The numbers are displayed to 2 decimal places, suitable for the display of pounds and pence.

   Now repeat this operation while the cells are still selected.

   Check in the option list if your copy of Excel has been set up to show the pound rather than the dollar currency symbol.

   If so you can select the option £###0.00.

   If not you can type this format directly into the Code box at the bottom of the screen.

   Hint. Always use the Format-Number option to add currency symbols. Do not enter currency symbols directly. If you do this then Excel will regard the values as text, not numbers, and be unable to use them in calculations.

5. **Inserting and Deleting Columns and Rows.** Click the column designator at the top of column B; this selects the whole column.

   Open the Edit menu and select Delete.

   Column B is deleted and subsequent columns are shifted to the left. All the cell references and formulae are automatically adjusted to reflect their new position.

Hint. Removing a blank column should cause no problems, but removing a column containing data and formulae obviously could. You can select Undo from the Edit column if you delete the wrong column or row.

Now let's insert an extra row; click the row designator for Row 2 – the whole row is selected.
Open the Edit menu and choose Insert. A new blank row is inserted.
The worksheet has a neater more balanced appearance and should now look like Figure 1.13

	A	B	C	D	E	F
1		PERSONAL FINANCES - TERM 1				
2						
3	INCOME	Week 1	Week 2	Week 3	Week 4	Week 5
4	Opening Bals.	0.00	1015.00	885.00	755.00	625.00
5	grant	500.00				
6	loan	400.00				
7	parents	300.00				
8	Total Income	1200.00	1015.00	885.00	755.00	625.00
9						
10	EXPENDITURE					
11	accomodation	60.00	60.00	60.00	60.00	60.00
12	food & Travel	30.00	35.00	35.00	35.00	35.00
13	books	75.00	15.00	15.00	15.00	15.00
14	other	20.00	20.00	20.00	20.00	20.00
15	Total Expenditure	185.00	130.00	130.00	130.00	130.00
16						
17	CLOSING BALS.	1015.00	885.00	755.00	625.00	495.00

Figure 1.13

6. **Centring the Title.** It would look neater to centre the title across columns A to F – the area of the worksheet that will eventually be printed.

Excel 3   **Excel 3 Users.** Click on cell A3 – the title appears in the formula bar at the top of the screen.
Move the pointer to the formula bar and click in front of the first letter of the title.
With the pointer located there, use the space bar to insert a few spaces in front of the title.
Click the tick box; you may have to repeat this operation until you are satisfied with the centring.
You can select Undo from the Edit menu to cancel the operation, or use the Delete and Backspace keys to remove excess spaces.

Excel 4   **Excel 4 Users.** Select row 1 from column A to column F, Open the Format menu and select the Alignment option.

A dialogue box appears, select the option 'Centre Across Selection', then click the OK button.

The title is centred across the columns selected. If you decide in the future to print out a different number of columns then you will need to re-centre the title.

There is also a Centre Across Columns Button on the Excel 4 toolbar – see key at the end of this chapter.

7.   **Adding Borders.** Borders can be used to mark off various sections of the worksheet and make it easier to read – see Figure 1.14.

First we will put a double border around the worksheet. Drag to select cells A1 to F17.

Open the Format menu and select Border. A dialogue box appears:

Select Outline in the Border box,

Select the double line icon in the Style box.

Finally click the OK button and then click to remove the highlight from the cells.

The worksheet is enclosed in a double box.

Now let's draw some single lines to mark off different sections of the worksheet.

Select cells A9 to F9.

Open the Format menu and select Border. The dialogue box opens.

Select the Bottom and single line options.

Click the OK button – this places a single line at the bottom of the cells.

Now draw another single line under cells A16 to F16.

Finally give the cells in column A a single right hand border.

Removing unwanted borders. Use the same commands, i.e. select the relevant cells, and select Border from the Format menu. Then click the relevant style box to remove the unwanted border.

Excel 4   **Excel 4 Users.** The Excel 4 Toolbar provides two buttons, the Outline Border tool and the Bottom Border tool which may be used instead – see the key at the end of this chapter.

8.   **Gridline Display.** The gridlines marking the cell boundaries can be turned off if desired to emphasise the borders that we have drawn.

Open the Options menu and choose Display. A dialogue box opens.

Click the Gridlines button – the X disappears as this option is deselected.

Click the OK button, and the gridlines disappear.

This will not prevent the gridlines displaying when the worksheet is printed – see Activity 9.

Your worksheet should now look like Figure 1.14.

	A	B	C	D	E	F
1		PERSONAL FINANCES - TERM 1				
2						
3	INCOME	Week 1	Week 2	Week 3	Week 4	Week 5
4	Opening Bals.	0.00	1015.00	885.00	755.00	625.00
5	grant	500.00				
6	loan	400.00				
7	parents	300.00				
8	Total Income	1200.00	1015.00	885.00	755.00	625.00
9						
10	EXPENDITURE					
11	accommodation	60.00	60.00	60.00	60.00	60.00
12	food & Travel	30.00	35.00	35.00	35.00	35.00
13	books	75.00	15.00	15.00	15.00	15.00
14	other	20.00	20.00	20.00	20.00	20.00
15	Total Expenditure	185.00	130.00	130.00	130.00	130.00
16						
17	CLOSING BALS.	1015.00	885.00	755.00	625.00	495.00

Figure 1.14

9. **Freezing Titles and Labels.** Before we print the worksheet we will add a note to the bottom. This means that the worksheet TERM1 will become too large to view all at once.

Before one scrolls to another part of the worksheet it is possible to 'freeze' both the titles and the column and row labels so that they are always in view, and so keep a track of what each row or column represents.

Look at the Up Arrow button on the vertical scroll bar; there is a thick black line just above it, the horizontal split box – see Figure 1.15.

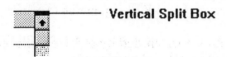
Vertical Split Box

Figure 1.15

Move the screen pointer onto this box. When located precisely, the pointer changes shape to a double-headed arrow.

Drag the box down to the bottom of row 3; a split box now divides off the top 3 rows.

Repeat this operation to freeze column A, using the vertical split box. This is located to the left of the scroll arrow in the bottom left-hand corner of the worksheet.

The worksheet is now split horizontally and vertically.

Excel 3   **Excel 3.** Open the Options menu and select the Freeze Panes option.

Excel 4   **Excel 4.** Open the Windows menu and select the Freeze Panes option.

Now try scrolling across and down; the column and row labels stay there as a permanent reference.

To Unfreeze Cells. Open the Options menu **(Excel 3)** or the Windows menu **(Excel 4)** and select Unfreeze Panes.
Then drag the split bars to either the top or left hand edge of the worksheet.

10. **Entering and Justifying Blocks of Text.** Although Excel does not offer full word processing facilities, blocks of text, such as brief notes, can be added to worksheets.
Activate cell B19 and type the line of text, 'Worksheet showing the income and expenditure', then press Enter. Activate cell B20 and type the next line, 'of the first 5 weeks of the Autumn Term.' Press Enter again.
To reorganise these 2 lines into shorter blocks of cells select the cell range B19 to D21 (9 cells).
Open the Format menu and select Justify.
The text is aligned into this new range of cells.
See also Activity 15.10 on using the Text Box Button to do this.

Activity 9. Printing a Worksheet

To print a worksheet properly you must give Excel instructions on what and how to print – which cells, number of copies, and so on.

1. **Setting the Print Area.** First select the entire worksheet area that you want to print – cells A1 to F21. Open the Options menu and select Set Print Area.
These cells are now surrounded by a dotted line. (this may not be fully visible due to the areas outlined previously)

2. **Page Setup.** Open the File menu and select the option Page Setup.
A dialogue Box appears.
It is usual to print a worksheet without the row and column headings and gridlines, if it is not too large or detailed.
Make sure that two boxes 'Row and Column Headings' and 'Cell Gridlines' are both unchecked, i.e. there is no 'X' in either of them.
Click the 'Center Horizontally' and 'Center Vertically' boxes. This will centre the printout on the page.
Now click the OK button.

3. **Other Page Settings.**
Your printer may offer the following settings, if so they will appear on the Page Setup dialogue box in black rather than pale grey.

❏ Orientation: Normally worksheets are printed in portrait, i.e. vertically down the page.
Wide worksheets can be printed in landscape – horizontally across the page.

❏ Paper: The current paper size is displayed, plus others supported by your printer.

❏ Reduce or Enlarge: You can adjust the size of the printed area to fit the paper size.

❏ Fit to Page: will automatically reduce the printed area to fit on one printed page.

❏ Margins: will vary the standard margin width.

The Printer. Make sure that the printer is:

❏ Switched on
❏ Set online – check switch and warning light
❏ Connected via cable to your computer
❏ has paper in it.

Check these in turn if the next section does not produce a printout.

4. **Printing.** Open the File menu and select the option Print.
A dialogue box appears. Alter the number of copies now if you want more than one.
It is also possible to specify which pages that you want to print if your worksheet extends over more than one page. We need not bother with this option for now.
Click the Preview box – an 'X' will appear in it.
Now click the OK button.
The Print Preview screen appears, showing how the worksheet will appear on the printed page.
There are various option along the top of the screen:

❏ Next and Previous are for multi-page worksheets.
❏ Margins displays the current margin settings.
❏ Print and Setup allow us to either proceed with printing or go back to the Page Setup menus.

Do not use any of these options for now.
Now move the screen pointer over the printed area – it changes to a magnifying glass shape. Click, and the area under the pointer is enlarged.
You can scroll around to look at other parts of the worksheet.
The Zoom button will return you to full page mode.
Now finally if you are happy with the print preview, click the Print button at the top of the screen.
(If you are not happy then the Close button will cancel printing)

The worksheet should start printing now.

Activity 10. Consolidation – Check your Progress

We are going to extend the TERM1 worksheet to cover a 10-week term.
I shall keep the instructions to a minimum, as you have already practised the operations involved.
References back to the relevant activities are given in brackets.

1. First select the week 5 column, i.e. cells F3–F17 and keep the mouse button pressed down.
   Drag across the worksheet to select the next 5 columns. These will hold the data for weeks 6-10. (Activity 6)

2. Now use the Fill Right command to copy the data across.
   Remember that you can always use the Undo command if you make a mistake.

3. Two minor amendments need to be made next.
   First amend the week numbers for weeks 6-10.
   You may also find that these new columns have a double right hand border – copied from the format for the week 5 column.
   Use the Format menu to remove or change unwanted cell borders. (Activity 8.7)
   Weeks 6-10 are reproduced as Appendix 1; check it with your version.

4. You will see that by the end of week 10 you are £155 in debt. The next Activity shows you how to try and solve this!

Activity 11. Testing Assumptions. What If?

A major advantage of worksheets, mentioned in the preface, is the ability to test out various assumptions by altering the values and noting the results. This 'what if' factor at its more sophisticated is called sensitivity analysis.
In our example we can find out what would happen if we cut down on expenditure.
We will alter our TERM1 worksheet model to see if we can end the term in the black.

1. Make the following two changes for weeks 6-10:
   The easiest way is to amend the relevant value for week 6, then Fill Right.

   ☐ Reduce the amount spent on books to zero.
   ☐ Spend £5 less on food and travel.

However you still end the term insolvent!
Save the worksheet at this point.

2. Let's assume that you find a part time job at £20 a week from week 7 onwards. This involves inserting an extra row to hold this new revenue category.
First select the row designator for row 7.
Open the Edit menu and select Insert.
A new row is inserted, label it 'Part Time Job'.
Now insert 20 for the last 4 weeks.
If entered correctly, this extra income means that you end the term with £25.
This is obviously only a simple example of building alternative models, based on different assumptions. In Chapter 4 we will use more sophisticated analysis tools.

3. We can save this optimistic model as a separate worksheet. Open the File menu and select Save as. (not Save)
Type in the file name A:\TERM1_V2 and click OK.

4. This new version of the worksheet is saved to disk as a separate file, and is displayed as the current worksheet. The original worksheet TERM1 can be recalled; open the File menu and you will see at listed at the bottom of the menu. Select the name and TERM1 is re-displayed.

Activity 12. Consolidation – Check your Progress

Make sure that the worksheet TERM1_V2 is displayed, then make the following changes:

1. From week 3 onwards Accommodation rises to £65 a week.

2. Your parents send you £30 for your birthday in week 8.

3. You want to go to an end of term celebration in week 10
Insert an appropriate amount in the 'Other' category for week 10 so that you end the term with £5.
Turn to Appendix 2 to check your calculations.

Activity 13. Creating and Using a Template

Let's discard the original worksheet TERM1, and use the worksheet TERM1_V2 as our preferred model for the term.

This type of model is much used in business, being in effect a cash flow forecast.

We can use it as a pattern or template for other college terms too; the income and expenditure, formulae and week headings will all remain the same, only the title and the actual values will change.

Although Excel allows you to create a special template worksheet, we shall use a simpler but equally effective method – modifying a worksheet, then saving the changes as a new worksheet.

1. Make sure that the worksheet TERM1_V2 is open.

2. Open the File menu and select Save as.

3. Type in the file name TERM2

4. Click the OK button. A new worksheet TERM2.XLS is created and opened ready for use. It is an exact copy of TERM1_V2 which is closed and remains unchanged.

5. Now make the following changes to TERM2 to reflect the different financial situation:

   a. You start the term with £55 overdraft; enter it as -55.
   b. You have a part-time job paying £25 per week for the whole 10 weeks. (use the Fill Right command as before)
   c. Your loan is only £300 this term.
   d. This term you spend £80 on books in week 1 only.
   e. Amend the title on row 1 to indicate Term 2.

   You should end the term with £45.

Activity 14. Deleting an Excel Document

From time to time you may need to discard unwanted documents – worksheets or charts. We now have three worksheets, TERM1.XLS, TERM1_V2.XLS and TERM2.XLS.

We do not need the original worksheet TERM1 and will delete it.

1. Open the File menu and select the Delete option.

A dialogue box appears; you may need to change to A drive first if this is where your documents are stored.
If so use the procedures in Activity 6, section 4.

2. Select the name TERM1.XLS from the list in the file box.
    Click the OK button.
    A dialogue box appears asking you to confirm the deletion.
    Check the file name very carefully.
    Click the Yes button to delete or the No button to cancel.
    Press the Close button now.

3. Now open the File menu again – you may see the name of the deleted file still listed at the bottom of the menu. However it cannot be opened; try to select it and you will get an error message.

4. Exit from Excel.

Activity 15. Consolidation – Averages and Percentages

In this activity we will recap on some of the skills that you have learnt and also find out how to calculate averages and percentages.

1. Open a new worksheet. If you have started a new Excel session then one is provided, otherwise open the File menu and select New.
    A dialogue box opens. The worksheet is the default option.
    Click the OK button.

2. Now create the worksheet shown in Figure 1.16.

	A	B	C	D	E
1		Insurance Sales - Ist Quarter			
2					
3		Motor	Life	Property	Total
4	Jan	1465	1243	2456	5164
5	Feb	1345	1456	1987	4788
6	Mar	1132	2310	1598	5040
7					
8	Qu'ly Average				
9	Qu'ly Total	3942	5009	6041	14992
10	% of Total				
11					

Figure 1.16

Format the worksheet as shown:

- ❏ title centred
- ❏ cell labels in bold
- ❏ values centred in cells
- ❏ numbers to 2 decimal places

3. Calculate the quarterly totals using SUM and Fill Right.

4. Save the worksheet as INS_SLS.XLS

5. We now wish to find the average sales for each type of insurance and place them in row 8.
Select cell B8 and enter the formula =AVERAGE(B4:B6) Click the tick box and the three cells are averaged. Use Fill Right to average the Life and Property categories too.

6. Now centre these three values in their cells and format them to two decimal places.

7. Next we will express the quarterly totals – cells B9 to D9 – as percentages of the total sales – cell E9.
Select cell B10 and enter the Formula =B9/$E$9
Click the tick box.
The quarterly total for motor insurance is shown as a decimal fraction of the overall quarterly total – 0.26 (the / is used for division).
Absolute and Relative References. The dollar signs in the formula that you have just used indicate an **absolute** cell reference. So far all the cell references that you have been using are **relative** references. This means that the position of any cells used in a formula are relative to the location of the cell where the formula is placed.
This means that Excel can adjust formulae when cells are copied, as we have seen.
However this would not work for the percentages that we have just calculated as they must all be based upon one fixed cell – E9. We do not want this cell value to be adjusted when we use the Fill Right command. The dollar signs in front of the column and row number make it into an absolute reference and prevent this happening.

8. Now to turn this into a percentage.
Make sure that cell B10 is still selected.
Open the Format menu and select Number

Excel 3 **Excel 3.** Locate the format 0.00% in the Format Number box – you may have to scroll to it. Click OK.

Excel 4. Click the Percentage option in the Category box. Select the format 0.00% from the Format Codes box. Click OK.

9. Motor insurance is now shown as 26.29% of total sales. Use the Fill Right command to show Life and Property as percentages too.

10. Now finally let's add a text box to the worksheet, explaining its function. The Text Box tool is provided on the standard Excel 3 toolbar; Excel 4 users may need to call it up using the Toolbars option on the Options menu – see the tool bar key at the end of this chapter.
    Click the Text Box tool – the pointer changes to cross hairs.
    Locate the screen pointer on the top left-hand corner of cell B13.
    Drag across and down to cell E15. The text box is now drawn.
    Enter the text, 'This worksheet shows an analysis of the three major insurance categories.'
    You will see that the text wraps automatically to the size of the box.
    Remove an unwanted box by clicking the border to select it.
    Then select Clear from the Edit menu.

11. Save and close the worksheet.

Activity 16. Excel 4 Users Only – AutoFormat

> AutoFormat allows you to format your worksheets automatically. It offers you 14 built-in formats to choose from, each one in five different styles.
> This allows you to format either ranges of cells or a complete worksheets in attractive, standardised formats, thereby saving the time and effort of designing your own.

1. Open the worksheet INS_SLS.XLS. Select all the cells in the worksheet.

2. Open the Format menu and select AutoFormat A dialogue box appears showing a sample worksheet.

3. Take some time to select all the various formats listed in the table; the sample changes to illustrate each different format selected.

4. Now select the Classic 3 format and then OK. Your worksheet is converted to the format chosen, but you will probably not be happy with its appearance, e.g. the columns are too wide.

5. Open the Edit menu and choose Undo AutoFormat – your worksheet is restored to its previous format.

Hint. Always use Undo immediately after making any unwanted change.

If all else fails then closing the worksheet without saving it will undo any disastrous mistakes – but you will also lose any other changes made since the worksheet was opened or saved.

6. Make sure that the worksheet cells are still selected and open the AutoFormat menu again.
    This time select the Classic 3 format from the table and then click the Options button.
    Six Formats to Apply are offered, initially all selected. Try deselecting and reselecting all of them and notice their effect on the sample.
    When a format is deselected, such as Border or Alignment, the existing ones continue to apply.

7. Now deselect the Font, Alignment and the Width/Height options then click OK.
    The worksheet is reformatted in the 'Classic 3' format, minus the options that we have deselected.

8. We could choose to save these changes using Save, or to save this format as a new version of the worksheet, using Save as, but we won't bother in this instance.
    Close the worksheet without saving.

Summary of Commands and Functions

Note: Menu commands show the menu name first, followed by the command to choose from the menu, e.g. Edit-Clear means open the Edit menu and select the Clear command.
Keyboard commands use the dash symbol to indicate that two keys should be pressed down at the same time, e.g. Ctrl-Home.

Keyboard Commands

Ctrl-Home	Go to cell A1
Ctrl-Down Arrow Key	Go to last row of the worksheet
Ctrl-Right Arrow Key	Go to last column of worksheet
F1	Select Help

Menu Commands

Edit-Clear	Delete cell contents
Edit-Copy	Copy selected cells
Edit-Cut	Remove selected cells
Edit-Fill Right	Copy selected cells into selected right hand columns
Edit-Undo	Undo previous operation
File-Close	Close current document
File-Exit	Exit Excel
File-Delete	Delete a document
File-Open	Retrieve an existing document
File-Page Setup	Amend page settings for printing
File-Paste	Insert cut or copied cells at a specified location
File-Print	Print document
File-Save	Save current document
Format-Alignment	Centre, left and right alignment
Format-AutoFormat **(Excel 4 only)**	Apply Excel built-in format
Format-Border	Add cell borders
Format-Column Width	Adjust column width
Format-Font	Embolden, Italics, character size and style
Format-Justify	Align text blocks
Format-Number	Format numbers, percentages etc.
Format-Row Height	Adjust row height
Formula-Goto	Go to a specified cell
Help	Select Help
Options-Display	do/do not display gridlines etc.
Options-Set Print Area	Set worksheet area to be printed
Options-Freeze Panes **(Excel 4 only)**	freeze row and column headings.
Window-Freeze Panes **(Excel 3 only)**	freeze row and column headings.

Functions

SUM()	Add a range of cells
AVERAGE()	Average range of cells

Excel 3 Toolbar

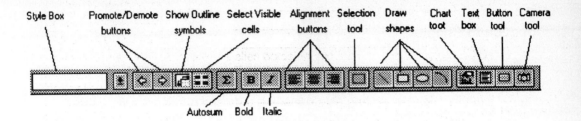

Excel 4 Toolbar

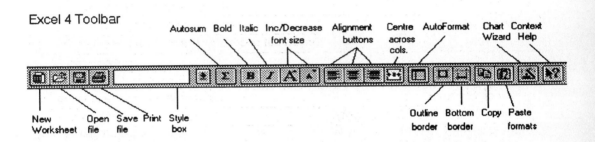

Figure 1.17

Chapter 2: Creating and Using Charts

Introduction to Chapter

In Chapter 1 you learnt some important worksheet skills – including entering data, using formulae to calculate, editing and formatting data and printing the worksheet.
You will be extending these skills further in Chapter 4, but for the moment we're going to use worksheet data to create charts and graphs
Excel lets you create a wide variety of different types – line graphs, pie charts, bar charts etc.

Summary of Skills covered

Skill	Activity	Skill	Activity
Active window – selecting	3	Chart Wizard	27
Area charts – creating	21	Column charts	24
Arrows – adding	11.3	Embedded Charts	27
Axis – changing	18	Gridlines – adding	23
Bar charts	24	Legend – adding	2
Charts – changing type	2	Legend – changing	17
Charts – copying	19	Line charts	14
Charts – creating	1	Multiple data ranges – selecting	15
Charts – deleting	20	Overlays – adding	25
Charts – formatting	11	Pasting values	22
Charts – printing	12	Patterns and colours	13
Charts – saving	5	Pie charts	2
Chart title – adding	8,16	Text – font and styles	11.2
Chart tool	27	Windows – sizing	4

Activity 1. Creating a Chart

1. If you are starting a new Excel session then open Excel as before; you will see a blank worksheet screen – see Figure 1.3.

2. Using the skills gained in Chapter 1, create the following simple worksheet. It shows the number of holidays sold by a travel company for various European countries.

	A	B	C	D	E	F
	EUROSLS.XLS					
1	**Sunfilled Holidays**					
2		**Holidays Sold - Europe**				
3						
4		**1st Quarter**	**2nd Quarter**	**3rd Quarter**	**4th Quarter**	**Total**
5						
6	**Italy**	85	99	200	93	477
7	**Spain**	150	246	355	145	896
8	**Portugal**	120	180	300	123	723
9	**Greece**	168	277	320	162	927
10	**France**	70	120	250	110	550
11						
12	**Total**	593	922	1425	633	3573

Figure 2.1

Format it as shown, i.e. data centred in columns, column widths adjusted, and headings and labels in bold.

3. Next total the first column in cell B12, using a formula.

4. Copy this formula to the next 4 cells.

5. Calculate the totals across in a similar way. As a check the grand total for all holidays should be 3573. If not check your data and your formulae!

6. Now save the worksheet as EUROSLS.
   We can now use this worksheet to create a variety of charts.

7. **Creating a chart**. First we will create a pie chart of the first quarter's sales. There are 4 simple steps:

   a. Select the cell range A6 – B10.

   b. Open the File menu and select New.

   c. Select Chart – see Figure 2.2.

   d. Select OK.

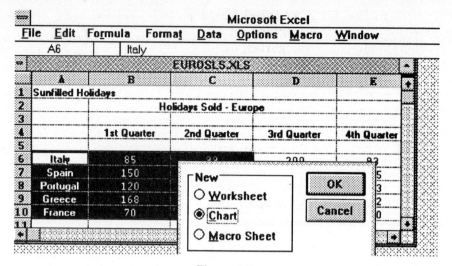

Figure 2.2

The chart produced should resemble Figure 2.3
It has not yet been saved to disk; it has been given the temporary name
CHART1.

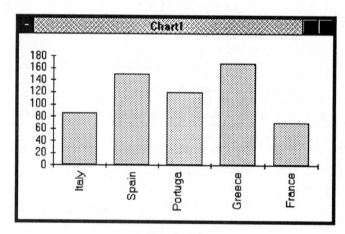

Figure 2.3

8. **Explanation of the Chart**. Excel has plotted a standard column chart,
    based on the data contained in cells A6 to B10. Let's study chart and work-
    sheet for a few moments, and see how Excel plots a chart; key terms that
    you should remember are in bold:-

    a. Each column on the chart represents one of the cell values that you
        selected on the worksheet, i.e. the values are different **data series**. In
        this simple chart there are 5 data series – the sales for each country –
        and 5 corresponding columns on the chart.

b. Excel takes the **text label** for each row – Italy, Spain etc – and places them on the **X or horizontal axis**.
These are the 5 categories; for this reason the X axis is also referred to as the **category axis**.

c. The numbers of holidays sold are plotted on the **Y or vertical axis**, also called the **value axis**.

d. Notice also that the menu bar has changed. It displays a new set of chart menu options.

Excel 4   e. **Excel 4** users have a special chart tool bar displayed at the bottom of the screen.

Activity 2. Changing the Chart type

1. Make sure that the column chart is still the active document, i.e. overlaying the worksheet.
Open the Gallery menu and Select Pie.
You are offered a choice of several types of pie chart. Chart type 1 is already selected

2. Select OK – the column chart is re-plotted as a pie chart. Pie charts are good for showing the relative contributions of various elements to the total 'pie'. However, the coloured sections need a key or legend to explain them.

3. Open the Chart menu and select Add Legend.
The legend appears on the chart.

Excel 4   4. **Excel 4 Users**. Click the various chart buttons on the chart tool bar at the bottom of the screen.
The data is re-drawn as various chart types. The toolbar is useful as it allows you to quickly review possible ways of charting your data. It also offers you Legend, Arrow tool and Text Box. However we will be mainly using the Gallery menu in this chapter as it offers you an even wider choice of charts.

Activity 3. Moving Between Chart and Worksheet

1. The pie chart and the worksheet are two separate documents.
At the moment the chart overlays the worksheet – it is the 'active window'

2. Click anywhere on the on the worksheet; it overlays the chart to become the active window.

3. If a window is completely hidden then you can use the Window menu. Open the Window menu and select CHART1 from the list offered.
    The pie chart becomes the active window again.

Activity 4. Resizing Windows

1. Let's now make the two windows smaller so that we can see chart and work-sheet alongside each other – see Figure 2.4.

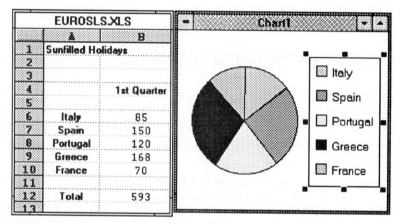

Figure 2.4

2. The method is basically the same as for worksheets.
    First make the worksheet the active window. Place the screen pointer on the bottom right hand corner of the worksheet – the cross-shaped screen pointer changes to a diagonal double-headed arrow.

3. Drag the screen pointer across to the left of the worksheet until only columns A and B are showing. Now place the screen pointer on the chart title (Chart1) and drag the chart to the right of the screen. If necessary re-size the chart in the same way as the worksheet. Do not overdo this as the chart dimensions can become rather 'squashed'.

4. The Window menu offers another way of resizing documents in order to dis-play them on the screen.
    Open the Window menu and select the Arrange option. Select the Vertical option from the dialogue box.

Activity 5. Saving a Chart

1. Open the File menu and select Save.

2. Make sure that the drive is set to A. (see Chapter 1, Activity 5)

3. Call the pie chart EUROPIE1.

4. Click OK. The chart is saved.
   Note that all charts are given the extension .XLC (this distinguishes them from worksheets with the .XLS extension)

Activity 6. Re-plotting a Chart

1. Now that Chart and Worksheet are both displayed we can show the dynamic relationship between them.
   Click the worksheet to activate it

2. Select cell B7 and amend the number of Spanish holidays to 500.
   The pie chart also changes to reflect this.

3. Open the Edit menu and select Undo Entry
   The pie chart returns to its previous shape.

Activity 7. Moving Pie Chart Segments

1. Activate the pie chart by clicking it.

2. Place the screen pointer on the segment denoting Portugal and click once – 'handles' appear on the segment.

3. Now drag the segment slightly away from the rest of the pie chart – this can be used for emphasis.

4. Move the screen pointer off the pie and click to turn off the handles.

Activity 8. Adding a Chart Title

1. Open the Chart menu and select Attach Text.

2. Select Chart Title from the next menu, then OK.
   A title box appears on the chart.

3.   Type 'European holidays – 1st Quarter' – at the moment this appears in the Formula Bar at the top of the screen.

4.   Click the Tick Box next to the Formula Bar.

5.   The Title now appears on the Screen – move the screen pointer away from the title and click to deselect the title.

Activity 9. Adding Values to a Chart

It can be difficult to judge the relative proportions of the pie chart segments unless the values are added.

1.   Open the Chart menu and select Attach Text.

2.   Select the Series and Data Point option from the dialogue box.

3.   Select the Point Number box.

4.   Type 1 and select OK. The value from the first cell in the data series – 85 for Italy is inserted.

5.   Move the screen pointer away from the new text and press the Esc key to turn off the handles.

6.   Repeat the steps used in above, to add the values to the pie segments for the remaining 4 countries.

It should now resemble Figure 2.5.

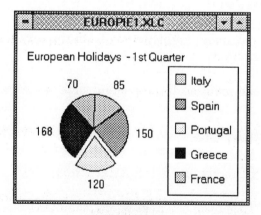

Figure 2.5

Activity 10. Saving a Chart Under a New Name

The Gallery menu allows you to change the active chart – EUROPIE1 – to another type. However this can override any special formatting that we may have already applied, e.g. the values that we have added and the organisation of the segments.
A way around this is to save it as a new chart under another name.

1. Make sure that EUROPIE1 is the active document.
    Open the Gallery menu and select the Pie option. Select the pie type that shows percentages for each segment. Click OK.

2. Using the **Save as** command (not **Save**) save this new version of the pie chart as EUROPIE2.
    Compare your result with Appendix 3 at the end of the book.

Activity 11. Formatting a Chart

1. Make sure that the pie chart EUROPIE1 is the active document.
    We are going to format the pie chart to improve its appearance further.

2. Changing Text Fonts and Style.
    First we will make the title more prominent.
    Move the screen pointer onto the title and click once.
    Selection 'handles' appear.
    Open the Format menu and select Font – a dialogue box appears.
    Choose Helvetica font (or another font if this is not available)
    Alter the size to 12 Point.
    Select Bold, then OK.
    The title will now change – click the title again to deselect it.
    n.b. Bold and Italic option are also available on the toolbars.

3. Adding Text and Arrows.
    The number of holidays sold for Portugal seems rather low for this quarter, so we'll add a comment to this segment.

    a. Open the Chart menu and select Add Arrow.

    b. First shorten the arrow if necessary by dragging the selection handle next to the tail. Next drag the arrow head next to the segment, then the tail of the arrow.

    c. If you make a mistake, click the arrow so the handles appear; then open the Chart menu and select Delete Arrows.

d. Adding text is simple; type the comment 'What went wrong?' The comment appears in the Formula Bar at the top of the screen.

e. Click the Tick Box next to the Entry Box. The comment now appears on the screen enclosed by handles.

f. Place the screen pointer on the comment and drag to move it next to the arrow. You can re-size the text by dragging the selection handles – try this.

g. Move the screen pointer away from the title and click to deselect the comment.

h. To edit the text, click it – the selection handles appear again. You can then either edit it in the text box, or delete it completely and start again.

4. If you are happy with the changes – compare your chart with Figure 2.6 – then save them.
If you are unhappy and want to begin the activity again then open the File menu and select Close.
Do not save the changes.
Then open the pie chart again and have another try!

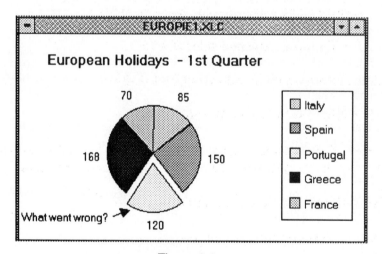

Figure 2.6

Activity 12. Printing a Chart

1. Make sure that the chart is the active window.
Open the File menu and select Print.

If the Print option is dimmed it is unavailable. Check that you have completed any operations – the tick box should not be displayed in the Formula bar (Excel 4 users can use the Print tool – see list at the end of Chapter 1)

2. A Print dialogue box opens; Select the number of copies.
    Now click the Preview then the OK button. The Print Preview screen shows the chart as it will appear on the printed page.
    If you are satisfied click the Print button, otherwise the Cancel button.

3. If nothing happens then check that:
    ❒ The printer is switched on – both at the mains and on the printer!
    ❒ The Online Switch on the printer is on.
    ❒ The cable from the computer to the back of the printer is connected.
    ❒ The paper supply/feed trays are OK.

Activity 13. Changing Chart Patterns and Colours

If you are using a black and white printer you may find that the coloured segments of the pie chart lack contrast when printed.

1. Click a segment to select it – the handles appear.

2. Open the Format menu and select Patterns

3. A dialogue box appears, allowing you to select:

    Border – different borders for the segments

    Area – Different combinations of colour and pattern for the segments. Black and white patterns are best for monochrome printers.

    Select suitable combinations and click OK.

4. Save and close the your pie charts.

Activity 14. Creating Line Charts

1. We are going to use data in the worksheet to create other type of chart – the line chart. Line charts are good for showing trends over time.
    Make sure that the worksheet EUROSLS is open.

2. Let's compare the sales for Italy and Spain for the 4 quarters.

Select cells A4 to E7.

3. Open the File menu and select New.

4. Select Chart, then OK. – the default column chart appears.

5. Open the Gallery menu and select Line.

6. Click OK to select the first type of line graph in the Gallery.
   The bar chart changes to a line graph.

7. Now open the Chart menu and select Add Legend.
   You may have noticed however – see Figure 2.7 – that the legend shows a third item – this is the blank row (5) that you selected on the worksheet.

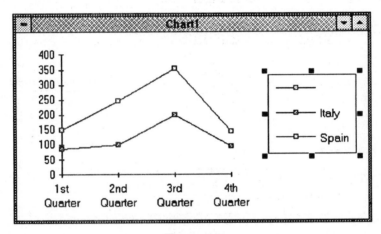

Figure 2.7

8. Re-create the chart by repeating the above steps, but this time only select cell range A6 to E7. The legend is now correct, i.e. only the data ranges for Italy and Spain are shown, but the 4 quarters are no longer shown along the X axis, only the numbers 1 – 4.
   This is because in order to omit the blank row, we were also obliged to omit row 4 containing the column headings.

9. We won't save the two charts created so far. Make each chart active in turn, then open the File menu and select Close.
   Close the charts without saving them.

Activity 15. Selecting Multiple Data Ranges

> To overcome the problem that we encountered in the previous activity, let's find out how to plot charts from cell ranges that are **not** adjacent – Italy and France.

1. Select the column headings B4 to E4.

2. Now hold down the Control key and select the 4 quarters for Italy – A6 to E6.
    Repeat these operations for the row for France.

3. Now create the line chart as before, adding a legend.
    Your chart should resemble Figure 2.8.

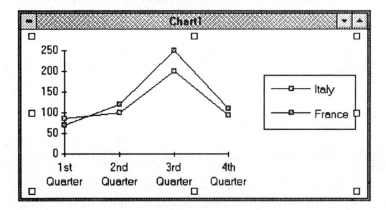

Figure 2.8

4. Add a suitable title to the chart – see previous Activity 8.

Save this chart as LINE1. Do not close the chart.

Activity 16. Adding Titles to Chart Axes

1. Move the screen pointer onto the horizontal axis first.

2. Click once and selection handles appear.

3. Open the Chart menu and select Attach Text.

4. Select Category Axis and click OK

5. Type the title PREVIOUS YEAR and press Enter. If necessary use the selection handles to move or resize the title.

6. Click elsewhere on the chart to deselect the axis.

7. Repeat the above operations to label the vertical or value axis HOLIDAYS SOLD, but this time do not deselect the axis.

8. Open the Format menu and select Text.
   A dialogue box appears.

Excel 3 9. **Excel 3**. Select Center in the Vertical Alignment box.
   Select Vertical Text, then OK.

Excel 4 10. **Excel 4**. Select the left column in the Orientation menu.

11. Save your completed chart again. You may also need to re-size the chart – see Activity 4.

Activity 17. Changing the Legend

1. Move the screen pointer onto the legend and click to select it – handles appear.

2. Open the Format menu and select Legend – a dialogue box appears.

3. Select Corner.

4. Next select the Patterns option.

Excel 3 5. **Excel 3**. Select Invisible Borders from the Borders menu, then OK.

Excel 4 6. **Excel 4**. Select None, then OK.

Activity 18. Changing the Value Axis

On the line chart LINE1 the values for Italy and France are very close at some points. This is because the scale is inappropriate for the range of values on the chart. We can change this default scale.

1. Move the screen pointer onto the vertical axis and click it to select it – selection handles appear.

2. Open the Format menu and select Scale; a dialogue box appears.

3. The values on the graph fall between the range 50 to 250.
   Type 50 in the Minimum box.
   Click OK.

4. The chart is replotted to show the new range.
   The data series for the 2 countries is more clearly separated.
   Open the Edit menu and choose the Undo and Re-do commands to review this.

Activity 19. Consolidation – Copying under a New Name

You may be undecided whether to use the original or rescaled version of the line chart.
We saw in Activity 10 that Excel allows you to copy the modified chart under a new name.
Save the chart LINE1 under the new name LINE2.
You now have 2 line charts, LINE1 and LINE2.
Check this by opening the File menu and selecting Open. You may need to scroll through the list of files.

Activity 20. Deleting a Chart

1. Open the File menu and Select Delete.

2. We've decided to keep LINE2, so let's delete LINE1.
   Select LINE1.XLS in the file list, then click OK.

3. A confirmation box appears.
   Check that the correct file is selected then click OK. The file is now deleted.

Activity 21. Area Charts

So far we've covered Pie and Line Charts. Area charts show both the amount of change over time, plus the sum of these changes. For example, in the case of European holidays we are not only interested in,
(i)   the performance for each country, but,
(ii)   its individual contribution to total holidays sold.

1. Select cells A4 to E10, i.e. all countries, all quarters.

2. Create a new chart as before, then open the Gallery menu and select Area. There are a number to choose from, try them all. i.e open the Gallery menu and select each area chart type in turn.

3. Now select the first chart type; the countries are labelled but not the quarters. Open the Chart menu and select Add Legend; the effect is rather crowded however.

4. Now open the Gallery menu again and choose the 5th area chart type that labels both countries and quarters – see Figure 2.9.

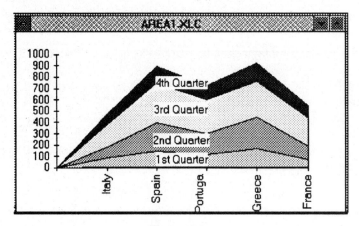

Figure 2.9

5. Now add a suitable title and label the axes as before.

6. Save the chart as AREA1.

Activity 22. Pasting Values from Worksheet to Chart.

Study the chart AREA1 carefully; it shows the 5 countries as the categories and the holidays sold in each quarter as the values. However it could be equally useful if the axes were reversed – the quarters formed the categories, (along the X axis) and the number of holidays the values (on the Y axis).

However Excel assumes that you want fewer data series than categories.

So, as the cells selected in the worksheet consist of 5 rows and 4 columns, (excluding cell labels) then the columns become the data series and the rows the categories.

We can get round this!

1. Activate the worksheet EUROSLS; this time select cells A4 to E8 (i.e. 3 countries only)

2. Create a new area chart from this cell range, the same type as before.
    As the cells selected consist of more columns than rows, (4:3, excluding blank rows and cell labels) then the column names in row 4 become the category names, and the row names in column A become data series names. You may need to think about this – compare your chart with Figure 2.9 above.

3. For a complete chart we need to insert the rows for the 2 remaining counties now.
    Activate the worksheet again and select A9 to E9.

4. Open the Edit menu and select Copy.

5. Re-activate the new chart – use the Window menu if necessary.

6. Open the Edit menu and select Paste.
    The values for Greece are pasted into the area chart as a new data series.

7. Repeat steps 4-6 for the 5th country – France.

8. Finally save the chart as AREA2 – it should resemble Figure 2.10.

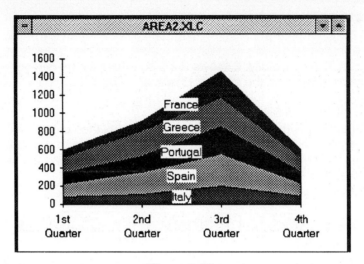

Figure 2.10

9. We now have 2 views of the same data:

    AREA1 – the countries are the categories, the values for quarters are plotted on the value axis.

    AREA2 – the quarters are categories , the values for the countries are plotted on the value axis.

    These techniques can be applied to other chart types.

Activity 23. Adding Gridlines

Adding gridlines to a chart can help us to read off the values more clearly.

1. Make sure that the chart AREA2 is the active window.
    Open the Chart menu and select Gridlines.

2. Select Major Gridlines for both the Category Axis and the Value Axis. Click OK. Gridlines can be deleted or modified by repeating the above steps.

Activity 24. Bar Charts and Column Charts

Bar charts and column charts show data values as a series of horizontal bars, or vertical columns. Both are suited to showing the relative sizes of 2 or more items; column charts are better for emphasising time series.

1. For these charts we're going to use another worksheet.
   See Figure 2.11.
   Format it as shown, and save it as BOOKSLS.

	A	B	C	D
1		Book Sales - Current Year		
2				
3	Month	No. Sold	Revenue	Advertising
4	Jan	850	2011	300
5	Feb	1050	3155	425
6	Mar	1175	3550	500
7	Apr	1430	4356	750
8	May	1710	5150	800

Figure 2.11

2. Select cells A3 – D6 and create a new chart.

3. Choose Bar from The Gallery menu.
   Accept the default bar type and add a legend.

4. This is the standard clustered bar chart, showing each month's value as a separate bar.

5. Open the Gallery menu again and select the 3rd type of bar chart – stacked bars.
   Save it as BAR1. (see Figure 2.12)

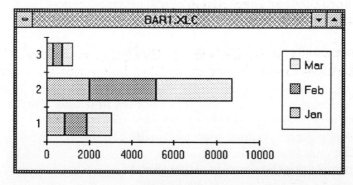

Figure 2.12

6. You may need to enlarge the chart to appreciate that each bar is the sum of the 3 smaller bars. This allows us to see the contribution of each month to the quarter's total for revenue, sales and advertising.

7. Return to the Gallery menu and select the fifth type of bar chart, the 100%, where all bars are shown of equal length. Add a title and label the Y axis and save this as BAR2.
    This type of bar chart shows the contribution of each month to an overall percentage, rather than the actual amounts.

8. Experiment now with the Column option in the Gallery menu. Try to produce the same three types of column charts – clustered, stacked and 100%. You need not save these.

Activity 25. Adding Overlays – Combination Charts

1. Make sure that worksheet BOOKSLS is the active window.

2. Select cells A3 to D8 and create a new chart.
    Accept the default column chart and add a Legend.

3. Move the screen pointer to one of the columns representing Advertising – selection handles appear.

4. Open the Chart menu and select Add Overlay; the data series for advertising is now plotted as a line chart.

5. This type of chart is called a combination chart, and is useful for emphasising relationships between different data series. In this case sales and revenue are still rising whilst the money spent on advertising has started to level off.

6. Save the chart as COMB1. Now open the Gallery menu and experiment with the other combination charts offered.

Activity 26 Consolidation – Check Your Progress

1. Using the worksheet BOOKSLS, create a column chart showing sales, revenue and advertising for the 3 months Feb, Mar and May.
    Use the techniques employed in Activity 15.
    Use overlapping columns, and add a title.
    Save the chart as COLUMN1.
    Compare it with the chart in Appendix 4.

2. Add a further column to the worksheet BOOKSLS, showing advertising as a percentage of sales for each month. Create a percentage pie chart showing this relationship; save it as BOOKPIE
Compare it with the chart in Appendix 5.

Activity 27. Embedded Charts

So far we have created separate chart documents. Excel also allows us to create embedded charts which form part of the worksheet. This is useful if you want to view or print a chart and worksheet on the same page.

Excel 3 Users – The Chart Tool.

1. Open the worksheet INS_SLS.
   Maximise the worksheet window.

2. Highlight the cell range A3 to C6.

3. Click the chart tool on the tool bar – see list at the end of Chapter 1.

4. Move the screen pointer back onto the worksheet – it is now cross-shaped. Drag the screen pointer across an empty area of worksheet, e.g. cell range F5 to H14. (press down the Shift key as well if you want the embedded chart to be square)

5. The embedded chart is created; it can be moved or re-sized using the selection handles.
   Chart and worksheet can be selected in turn by clicking.

6. To edit the chart double click it; the chart menu bar will then be displayed and the chart can be edited as if it were a separate document.

7. A chart can be deleted – select it and choose the Clear option from the Edit menu.

8. You can save or print the chart now as part of the worksheet.

Excel 4 Users – Chart Wizard.

Chart Wizard allows you to create simple charts by guiding you through 5 dialogue boxes. If you have completed earlier parts of the chapter you will find them straightforward.

1. Open the worksheet INS_SLS.
   Maximise the worksheet window.

2. Highlight the cell range A3 to D6.

3. Click the Chart Wizard button on the tool bar – see list at the end of Chapter 1.

4. Move the screen pointer back onto the worksheet – it is now cross-shaped.
   Drag the screen pointer across an empty area of worksheet, e.g. cell range B11 to E18. (press down the Shift key as well if you want the embedded chart to be square)

5. 'Chart Wizard – Step 1 of 5' is displayed.
   (At each step you have the option of cancelling, getting help, going back a step, or going on to the next step) Accept the range of cells offered by clicking the Next button.

   'Chart Wizard – Step 2 of 5' is displayed.
   Choose a suitable chart type, e.g. 3D Line.
   Click the Next button.

   'Chart Wizard – Step 3 of 5' is displayed.
   Choose a suitable format and click the Next button.

   'Chart Wizard – Step 4 of 5' is displayed.
   You can now alter certain basic chart parameters.
   Try these and note the result, then click the Next button.

   'Chart Wizard – Step 5 of 5' is displayed.
   You can add Legend and titles at this stage.
   Do this and click OK.

6. The embedded chart is created; it can be moved or re-sized using the selection handles.
   Chart and worksheet can be selected in turn by clicking.

7. To edit the chart double click it; the chart menu bar will then be displayed and the chart can be edited as if it were a separate document.

8. A chart can be deleted – select it and choose the Clear option from the Edit menu.

9. You can save or print the chart now as part of the worksheet.

Summary of Commands

Note: Menu commands show the menu name first, followed by the command to choose from the menu, e.g. Edit-Clear means open the Edit menu and select the Clear command.

Chart-Add legend	Add legend to chart
Chart-Add Arrow	Add arrow to chart
Chart-Add Overlay	Add overlay to chart
Chart-Attach Text	Attach text or values to chart
Chart-Gridlines	Add gridlines to chart
File-Delete	Delete a chart
File-New-Chart	Create new chart from selected cells
Format-Font	Change font of selected text
Format-Patterns	Change chart patterns and colours
Format-Scale	Change scale of chart axis
Format-Legend	Change position/borders of Legend
Gallery-[chart type]	Change chart type
Window-[document name]	Make document active
Window-Arrange	Arrange documents on screen

Chapter 3: Creating and Using a Database

Introduction to the Chapter

In Chapters 2 and 3 we covered worksheets and charts, the first two components of Excel.

This chapter covers the third component, databases. Businesses use databases to store and retrieve records of all types – customers, employees, goods in stock, etc.

The software package used to create and run databases is called a database management system or DBMS.

Excel does not offer all the features of a special-purpose DBMS such as dBASE or Paradox, but its column and row structure lets you perform straightforward tasks such as:

❑ finding individual records

❑ adding new records

❑ editing existing records

❑ deleting records

More complex tasks are also possible, such as sorting records into a different order, or extracting all records meeting a particular search criterion.

Figure 3.1 is an example of a simple database that records customer orders. We can use it to introduce certain key database terms.

	A	B	C	D	E
			ORDERS.XLS		
	Order No.	Order Date	Co. Ref	Co. Name	Value
1					
2	14000	10-Mar	1453	Wilson Garages	3200.44
3	14001	8-Mar	2413	Patel Industries	1466.00
4	14002	11-Mar	1453	Wilson Garages	98.76
5	14003	11-Mar	1289	Marsden Products	4456.00
6	14004	10-Mar	2413	Patel Industries	567.00
7	14005	11-Mar	955	Tilley Transport	1678.09
8	14006	10-Mar	2375	Patel Kitchens	55.44
9	14007	9-Mar	1453	Wilson Garages	2654.00
10	14008	12-Mar	2245	Goldfield Stables	123.85
11	14009	12-Mar	1289	Marsden Products	1652.54

Figure 3.1

Record. There is an entry for each order.
Each entry is called a record and takes up a row.

Field. Each record contains the same 5 fields or items of information – Order No, Order Date, Co. Ref, Co. name and Value. Each field takes up a column.

The first row of the database contains the **field names**, the other rows contain the actual data – the **field values**.

Database. At the moment our database consists of a **range** of 10 records.

Database Rules in Excel

Database size. A database can be as large as the entire worksheet, but cannot occupy more than one worksheet.

Fields / Field names. The top row of the database must contain field names. Field names must consist of letters only, not numbers, blank cells etc.

Field names can be up to 256 characters long and must be unique

Records. Every record must have the same fields, but fields can be left blank. Do not enter extra blanks at the start of fields.

Capitalization. Excel ignores upper or lower case when searching or sorting the database, so you may use either, e.g.'SMITH', 'smith' or 'Smith'.

Summary of Skills Covered

Skill	Activity	Skill	Activity
'AND' in Searching	5.10	Records – deleting	4.3
Calculated fields – creating	3	Records – editing	4.5
Database – defining	4,6	Records – extracting	6
Data Forms – using	4	Records – searching	4 and 5
Data Series – creating	1.3	Records – sorting	2
Dates – formatting	1.4	Search Criteria – using	5
Extracting records	6	Statistical Functions – using	7
'OR' in Searching	5.10	Wildcard Searching	5.9

Activity 1.   Building the Database

It is essential to plan the structure of a database before you create it. The items of information that you need will determine what fields you include. For example, Figure 3.1 shows a database set up to record customer orders. We therefore need to know not only the customer details – name and reference code – but also the order details – date, reference code and value. Each of these is given its own field and can be processed separately.

Notice that we also have implicitly decided what not to store e.g. the customer address – which would probably be stored in a customer database rather than an order database.

1. The first step after planning the structure is inserting the field names shown in Figure 3.1.

    Make sure that you have a new blank worksheet displayed, then type in the 5 field names shown as column headings. Use the right arrow key to move across the columns.

    Widen the columns where necessary, and centre and embolden the field names.

2. Now enter the Co. Ref and Co. Name fields as shown in columns C and D of Figure 3.1.

    Next enter the order values in the Value column.

    Don't enter .00 after a value if there are no pence, so, e.g., in the case of cell E3, just enter the value 1466.

3. Now we will format the values to 2 decimal places

    Select the 10 value fields – cell range E2 to E11. Open the Format menu and select the Number option. Select the 0.00 option and click the OK button.

4. The Order no. field is a numeric sequence – increasing by 1 for every new order.

    We can use the Data Series command when numbers or dates in adjacent cells increase (or decrease) by a constant factor.

    Enter the start value 14000 in cell A2, then select the whole range, A2 to A11.

    Open the Data menu and select the Series option.

    A Dialogue box appears, make sure that the following options are selected, as shown in Figure 3.2.

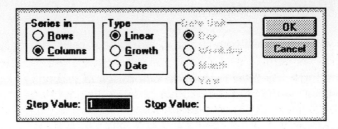

Figure 3.2

Series in Columns: the data series will occupy a column

Linear: the progression will be linear

Step value 1: the numbers will increase by 1 each time (for weekly dates you would step value 7)

Click the OK button and the column is filled with the order numbers 14000-14009.

5. **Entering the Order Date**. Excel allows dates to be entered in a variety of formats and in most cases will automatically assign the correct date format. Enter the first date field as 10mar and press Enter. Excel automatically converts it to the date format 10-Mar.
Enter the remaining field values in a similar way.
Look at the status bar at the top of the screen as you do this.
Irrespective of the date format in the cells Excel displays dates in a US numeric format, e.g. 3/10/92.

6. Finally centre the field values for the Order No, Order Date and Co. Name fields.
The database should now resemble Figure 3.1 above.

7. Save the database as ORDERS.
You will see that it is assigned the usual worksheet extension .XLS.

Activity 2. Sorting the Database

A common business need is to present the same information in a variety of ways, e.g. in order number sequence, (as at present) or in order date sequence.
Sorting involves rearranging the records in a new physical sequence, and speeds up search time once a database gets over a certain length.
The field used to sort the database is called the **sort key** or **key field**; we can sort the database in order of any field or fields.

Rules and Hints for Sorting.

Sorting will work with any range of worksheet cells, not only databases.

Do not include any field **names** in the range of records to be sorted – otherwise they will get sorted too.

Order of Sorting: field values are sorted in the following order:
☐ Numbers
☐ Text
☐ Logical Values
☐ Error Values
☐ Blanks

You can always undo an unsuccessful sort by selecting Undo Sort from the Edit menu, provided that you do so immediately.

All the fields in the database, i.e. all columns, must be included in the sort, otherwise any fields omitted from the sort will remain in the same sequence and become attached to the wrong records.

1. Let's sort the customer orders into date sequence first.
    Select cells A2 to E11 – all fields, all records.
    Open the Data menu and select Sort.
    The Sort dialogue box appears.
    If necessary, locate the screen pointer on the box title and drag the box down a little so that the database is visible.

2. Complete the dialogue box as follows:

    Sort by: leave this selected as Rows; each row is a single record, and sorting by rows keeps the records intact.

    1st Key: We want to sort by the field values in column B – Order Date.

    Click anywhere on column B, e.g. cell B1. The cell is enclosed with a moving border, and the reference $B$1 appears in the 1st Key box.
    The screen should now resemble Figure 3.3

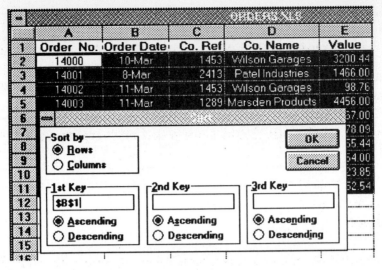

Figure 3.3

Click the OK button and the ten records are sorted in a new sequence.

3. **Consolidation – Resorting record**s. A sort can be changed by either selecting Undo Sort from the Edit menu, or by another sort operation.
Using sections 1 and 2 as a guide, sort the ten records by Co. Name.
Notice that strict alphabetical sequence is followed, the record for Patel Industries is placed before Patel Kitchens.

4. **Sorting by more than one key**. Let's sort the records in reverse date sequence, within Co. Name.
This means that all the records for, e.g. Wilson Garages, are grouped together, with the latest orders displayed first. This involves two keys; Co. Name as the primary key and Order Date as the secondary key.
Make sure that the entire database range is selected as before (except for the field names) and issue the Sort command.
Complete the Sort dialogue box as follows:

a. Select Co. Name. as the 1st Key.

b. Now click the 2nd Key dialogue box to activate it.

c. Click the Order Date column – the cell reference in the 2nd Key box should now read $B$1.

d. Click the Descending button in the 2nd Key box.

e. Finally click the OK button.

The ORDERS database should now resemble Figure 3.4

	A	B	C	D	E
	Order No.	Order Date	Co. Ref	Co. Name	Value
2	14008	12-Mar	2245	Goldfield Stables	123.85
3	14009	12-Mar	1289	Marsden Products	1652.54
4	14003	11-Mar	1289	Marsden Products	4456.00
5	14004	10-Mar	2413	Patel Industries	567.00
6	14001	8-Mar	2413	Patel Industries	1466.00
7	14006	10-Mar	2375	Patel Kitchens	55.44
8	14005	11-Mar	945	Tilley Transport	1678.09
9	14002	11-Mar	1453	Wilson Garages	98.76
10	14000	10-Mar	1453	Wilson Garages	3200.44
11	14007	9-Mar	1453	Wilson Garages	2654.00

Figure 3.4

5. **Consolidation**. Try sorting the order records as follows,

   a. In descending order of value, i.e. largest orders first.

   b. By Co. Ref. in ascending date order – compare your result with Appendix 6.

Activity 3. Creating New Fields by Calculation

> We are going to add two new fields to the database:
> a.   The VAT field will hold the 17.5% VAT to be added to the value of an order.
> b.   The Total field which will hold the VAT field added to the order value field.
> These new fields can both be calculated by formulae in the usual way.

1. Make sure that the worksheet ORDERS is open. Add the two new field names, VAT and Total, in cells F1 and G1. Centre them in their cells.

2. VAT is 17.5% of Value; move to cell F2 and apply the formula =E2*0.175 Now copy this formula to the rest of the VAT fields using the Fill Down command. (* is the multiplication sign.)

3. Now calculate the first Total field by adding the Vat field to the Value field. Fill Down again.

4. Format the two new fields to 2 decimal places.

5. Calculated fields can be searched and sorted in the same way as any other fields. To demonstrate this, sort the database by the Total field (ascending order)

Your database should now resemble Figure 3.5

	A	B	C	D	E	F	G
1	Order No.	Order Date	Co. Ref	Co. Name	Value	VAT	Total
2	14006	10-Mar	2375	Patel Kitchens	55.44	9.70	65.14
3	14002	11-Mar	1453	Wilson Garages	98.76	17.28	116.04
4	14008	12-Mar	2245	Goldfield Stables	123.85	21.67	145.52
5	14004	10-Mar	2413	Patel Industries	567.00	99.23	666.23
6	14001	8-Mar	2413	Patel Industries	1466.00	256.55	1722.55
7	14009	12-Mar	1289	Marsden Products	1652.54	289.19	1941.73
8	14005	11-Mar	955	Tilley Transport	1678.09	293.67	1971.76
9	14007	9-Mar	1453	Wilson Garages	2654.00	464.45	3118.45
10	14000	10-Mar	1453	Wilson Garages	3200.44	560.08	3760.52
11	14003	11-Mar	1289	Marsden Products	4456.00	779.80	5235.80
12							

Figure 3.5

Activity 4. Database Maintenance Using a Data Form

Obviously all databases need updating; as information changes; records need adding, deleting and amending.
You can use a special Excel data form to simplify the searching and updating process.

1. Make sure that the ORDERS worksheet is open for use.
    The first step is to define the worksheet as a database. Select all the cells, i.e. the 10 records **plus** the field headings in row 1.
    Open the Data menu and select the option Set Database. The database is now defined.
    Note. You will need to redefine the database range in this way every time records are added to or deleted from the database.

2. Open the Data menu again and select the Form command.

A data form is displayed. On the left hand side of the form are shown the field names and fields of the first record – see Figure 3.6.

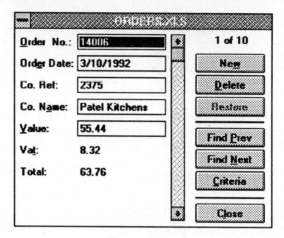

Figure 3.6

3. Let's carry out some key database tasks using the command buttons on the right hand side of the data form:

    Find Next button. Click this to scroll forward in the database a record at a time.
    Notice how the field values change and the Record Counter displays the current record – 2 of 10, 3 of 10 etc.

    Find Prev. button. Click this to scroll backwards in the database.

    Scroll Bar. Moves between records more rapidly.
    Move to the Last record in the database – 10 of 10.

    Delete button. Click it once.
    A message warns you that 'Displayed record will be deleted permanently'.
    Click the Cancel button. (records deleted with a data form cannot be restored, so make sure that you really want to delete a record before deleting it)

    Criteria button. Allows you to locate records by named criteria. You will be learning this in more detail in later sections.

4. Try these simple searches now:

    a. Scroll back to the first record and click the Criteria button. A blank record is displayed.
        Enter your first criterion, Patel, in the Co. Name field, then click the Find Next button.
        The first record matching this search criterion is displayed; press the Find Next button again to view any further matches.

There are 3 records in all. Notice that both Patel companies are located – we would need to enter the complete company name to narrow the search further.
A 'bleep' informs you when the last matching record is displayed.
Press the Find Prev. button to scroll back again.

b. Press the Criteria button again. Patel is still displayed in the Co. Name field.
Use the Tab key to move to the Value field and enter the second criterion <1000
Click the Find Next button.
Two records match the combined criteria, i.e. company name = Patel and order value less than £1000.
Click the Criteria button to return to the Data form.

5. **Editing Data**. The first 5 data fields can be edited, but the two calculated fields, VAT and Total, cannot be changed.
Their data is produced by formulae which cannot be overwritten. This is why the data in these 2 fields is not enclosed in boxes – see Figure 3.6.
Using the data form find the record for order number 14005 and amend the Co. Ref to 955.
Important Note. Changes to a record made using a data form are saved permanently as soon as you move to another record, even though no specific Save command has been given.
The Restore button will only undo the change providing you press it **before** you move to another record.

6. Press the Close button to exit from the data form.

7. **Consolidation**. Using the operations you have just learned, open the data form again and use the Criteria button to locate records matching the following conditions:

a. Order Total greater than or equal to 3000 (>=)

b. Orders placed before 10-Mar

c. Co. Ref = 1289

Activity 5. More Complex Searches

The data form that we used in the previous activity has limited search facilities. It can only display one record at a time, and we cannot use 'or' conditions such as > 1000 or < 2000 in a data form field.

By setting up our search criteria on the worksheet itself we can perform these more complex type of searches.

1. We will conduct these searches in a new database that holds details of voluntary helpers who act as guides, gardeners, drivers etc. at heritage sites in various areas.

	A	B	C	D	E	F
	SURNAME	FORENAME	AREA	JOB	AGE	AVAILABILITY
2	Morrison	James	Winton	Driver	33	12-Jul
3	Beattie	Joanna	Wimborne	Gardener	65	13-Jul
4	Maxwell	Lucy	Ringwood	Guide	34	20-Jul
5	Sewill	Pamela	Winton	Driver	39	23-Jul
6	Hall	Richard	Poole	Canteen	54	22-Jul
7	Hennell	Janice	Poole	Kitchen	50	26-Jul
8	Goldfield	Cheryl	Boscombe	Guide	34	30-Jul
9	Wilson	Jim	Wimborne	Warden	43	30-Jul
10	Muir	John	Redhill	Warden	16	30-Jul
11	Franks	Liz	Mudeford	Kitchen	68	2-Aug
12	Rolfe	Drusilla	Poole	Guide	20	2-Aug
13	Hurne	Gerrard	Wallisdown	Gardener	40	4-Aug
14	Main	Graham	Downton	Driver	25	30-Jul
15	Ali	Kate	Ringwood	Canteen	66	5-Aug

Figure 3.7

Create a new worksheet, format it as shown, and save it as HELPERS.

2. The first step, as before, is to define the worksheet cells as a database. Select all the cells, i.e. the 14 records **and** the field headings on row 1. Open the Data menu and select the option Set Database. The database is now defined.

3. The next step is to set up the search criteria. Select all the 6 field names in row 1. Using the Edit menu, copy and paste these cells down to row 17.

4. When you have copied the cells, select them, **plus** the same number of cells in the row underneath.

You should now have selected cell range A17 to F18 – see Figure 3.8.

	A	B	C	D	E	F	G
1	SURNAME	FORENAME	AREA	JOB	AGE	AVAILABILITY	
2	Morrison	James	Winton	Driver	33	12-Jul	
3	Beattie	Joanna	Wimborne	Gardener	65	13-Jul	
4	Maxwell	Lucy	Ringwood	Guide	34	20-Jul	
5	Sewill	Pamela	Winton	Driver	39	23-Jul	
6	Hall	Richard	Poole	Canteen	54	22-Jul	
7	Hennell	Janice	Poole	Kitchen	50	26-Jul	
8	Goldfield	Cheryl	Boscombe	Guide	34	30-Jul	
9	Wilson	Jim	Wimborne	Warden	43	30-Jul	
10	Muir	John	Redhill	Warden	16	30-Jul	
11	Franks	Liz	Mudeford	Kitchen	68	2-Aug	
12	Rolfe	Drusilla	Poole	Guide	20	2-Aug	
13	Hume	Gerrard	Wallisdown	Gardener	40	4-Aug	
14	Main	Graham	Downton	Driver	25	30-Jul	
15	Ali	Kate	Ringwood	Canteen	66	5-Aug	
16							
17	SURNAME	FORENAME	AREA	JOB	AGE	AVAILABILITY	
18							

Figure 3.8

Open the Data menu and select the option Set Criteria.
You have now created a criteria range; the first row of cells contains the field names, the second row of blank cells are for you to enter your search criteria.
You merely enter your criteria under the field that you want to search.

5. Let's select all the records for drivers first.
   Enter the search term driver in cell D18 underneath the field name Job.
   Remember to press Enter or click the tick box to enter this search term.
   Open the Data menu and select the Find option.
   You are now in Find mode; the scroll bar changes its function (and appearance) slightly in Find mode.
   The first matching record for helper Morrison is selected. Click on the scroll down arrow and the next matching record is displayed and so on.
   The scroll up arrow reverses the search direction.
   To end the search, either click anywhere on the worksheet, or open the Data menu and select Exit Find.

6. Now add a further search criterion Winton in cell C18.
   Use the Find option again; only two drivers are available in this area.

7. **Comparison Operators**. The following 6 operators can be used in searching the database:
   = equal to (not needed on its own)
   < less than
   > greater than

71

        <> not equal to
        <= less than or equal to
        >= greater than or equal to

Use them to make the following three searches:
- ❏ Helpers living in Wimborne (no operator needed)
- ❏ Helpers aged 50 or over
- ❏ Poole helpers available before 25th July.

8. **Search Hints**.
   - ❏ Erase previous search conditions using the Clear command or the Back-space key.
   - ❏ Press Enter after entering the search criterion.
   - ❏ Exit from Find mode before starting the next search.

9. **Wildcard Searching**. The * and ? characters can be used to stand for one or more characters.
   Try the following three searches:

   a. Enter *ton as a search condition under the area field. Records for both Winton and Downton are located.
   The * character can substitute for any combination of adjacent characters.

   b. Enter the search condition Ger?ard under the forename field.
   If we are unsure if the forename 'Gerrard' is spelled with a single or double 'r', the ? character can be used to substitute for a single character.
   The record for Gerrard Hurne will be located.

   c. Enter the search condition Wi under the Area field. Records for both Wimborne and Winton are located, i.e. there is no need to use a wildcard character if you can supply the starting characters of the search criterion.

10. **'And' vs. 'Or'**. When we used more than one search criterion we have implicitly used the AND condition; i.e. both conditions needed to be met for a record to be retrieved, e.g. Poole area AND available 25th July.
    We also need to search using the OR condition, e.g. Poole or Ringwood area, age under 20 or over 40.
    To use OR we need to reset the criteria range.
    Select the 6 field name cells A17 to F17, **plus 2 rows of 6 cells immediately beneath them** – see Figure 3.9.

	A	B	C	D	E	F
4	Maxwell	Lucy	Ringwood	Guide	34	20-Jul
5	Sewill	Pamela	Winton	Driver	39	23-Jul
6	Hall	Richard	Poole	Canteen	54	22-Jul
7	Hennell	Janice	Poole	Kitchen	50	26-Jul
8	Goldfield	Cheryl	Boscombe	Guide	34	30-Jul
9	Wilson	Jim	Wimborne	Warden	43	30-Jul
10	Muir	John	Redhill	Warden	16	30-Jul
11	Franks	Liz	Mudeford	Kitchen	68	2-Aug
12	Rolfe	Drusilla	Poole	Guide	20	2-Aug
13	Hurne	Gerrard	Wallisdown	Gardener	40	4-Aug
14	Main	Graham	Downton	Driver	25	30-Jul
15	Ali	Kate	Ringwood	Canteen	66	5-Aug
16						
17	SURNAME	FORENAME	AREA	JOB	AGE	AVAILABILITY
18						
19						

Figure 3.9

There should be 18 cells selected in all, from A17 to F19. Now open the Data menu and select Set Criteria.

11. Let's retrieve records for areas Boscombe or Ringwood.
    Enter Boscombe in the first cell below the Area criterion cell (C18).
    Enter Ringwood in the second cell below the Area criterion cell (C19).
    Now issue the Find command; records for either Boscombe or Ringwood are located.

12. We can now make a more complex search – guides for Ringwood or wardens for Redhill. The logic is (guide AND Ringwood) OR (warden AND Redhill). Enter the search criteria as shown in figure 3.10.

	A	B	C	D	E	F
12	Rolfe	Drusilla	Poole	Guide	20	2-Aug
13	Hurne	Gerrard	Wallisdown	Gardener	40	4-Aug
14	Main	Graham	Downton	Driver	25	30-Jul
15	Ali	Kate	Ringwood	Canteen	66	5-Aug
16						
17	SURNAME	FORENAME	AREA	JOB	AGE	AVAILABILITY
18			ringwood	guide		
19			redhill	warden		

Figure 3.10

The Find command will find records matching either set of criteria.

13. Now try the following searches:

    a.   Helpers over 60 or under 21.

    b.   Guides before 21 July or after 1st August. (you will have to enter the job criterion twice – on both rows)

Activity 6. Extracting Records from the Database

We now know how to find records using search criteria. Once a database gets to a certain length, we might find it useful to extract certain records and copy them to another part of the worksheet.

We will use the ORDERS database, used in activities 2 and 3, to practise this.

Extracting data involves three preliminary steps, the first two are the same ones we used to search a database.

1.   **Set the Database**. Open the worksheet ORDERS.XLS and select the whole database, including the field names.
Open the Data menu and select Set Database.
The worksheet should be re-defined as a database every time it is opened for use in case records have been added or deleted.

2.   **Set Criteria**. Copy the field names from row 1 and paste them to row 13.
These field names now need to be defined as our search criteria.
Select them, plus the 7 cells underneath them, ie. cell range A13 to G14.
Open the Data menu and select Set Criteria.

3.   **Define the Extract Range**. This tells Excel where to put the records after they have been extracted from the database.
The extract range, like the criteria range requires a row of field names matching those in the database.
Copy the field names once again; this time to row 16.
Make sure that this row of cells is still selected. Open the Data menu and select Set Extract.
Your worksheet will now resemble Figure 3.11.

	A	B	C	D	E	F	G
1	Order No.	Order Date	Co. Ref	Co. Name	Value	Vat	Total
2	14001	8-Mar	2413	Patel Industries	1466.00	256.55	1722.55
3	14007	9-Mar	1453	Wilson Garages	2654.00	464.45	3118.45
4	14006	10-Mar	2375	Patel Kitchens	55.44	9.70	65.14
5	14004	10-Mar	2413	Patel Industries	567.00	99.23	666.23
6	14000	10-Mar	1453	Wilson Garages	3200.44	560.08	3760.52
7	14002	11-Mar	1453	Wilson Garages	98.76	17.28	116.04
8	14005	11-Mar	955	Tilley Transport	1678.09	293.67	1971.76
9	14003	11-Mar	1289	Marsden Products	4456.00	779.80	5235.80
10	14008	12-Mar	2245	Goldfield Stables	123.85	21.67	145.52
11	14009	12-Mar	1289	Marsden Products	1652.54	289.19	1941.73
12							
13	Order No.	Order Date	Co. Ref	Co. Name	Value	Vat	Total
14							
15							
16	Order No.	Order Date	Co. Ref	Co. Name	Value	Vat	Total
17							

Figure 3.11

Important Note. Any information already underneath the field names of the extract range will be overwritten by the extracted data. It will be permanently lost, as you cannot undo an extract command (unless you exit the worksheet without saving it)

So either be careful where you place the extract range, or limit it to a definite number of rows.

This can be done by selecting that number of rows in addition to the field names when you define the extract range.

4. **Extracting Records**. Let's extract all records totalling less than £1000.
   Move to cell G14 and enter the criterion <1000
   Open the Data menu and select Extract.
   A dialogue box appears offering the choice to 'Extract Unique Records Only.' This allows you to eliminate any duplicate records from the selection.
   Click OK to select all records.
   All the records matching the search criterion (Total < 1000) are extracted and copied below the extract range, row 16.

5. Clear the search condition from cell C14 and the extracted records from row 17 and below.
   Now extract all the records where the order date is on or before 10-Mar.

6. **Extracting Partial Records**. Instead of extracting the full record, you can extract certain fields only.
   Clear the original extract range and extracted records plus any search criteria.
   Copy the three field names Order No., Co. Name, and Value into cells A16 to A18.

75

Select these three cells and define them as the new extract range, using the Data menu as before.

Enter the search criterion >0 in cell A14, then open the Data menu and select Extract.

All 10 records are extracted and copied, but only the 3 fields that you specified.

7. **Consolidation**. Open the HELPERS worksheet and extract the following records:

All members aged 50 or over

All members aged 50 or over available on or after 26-Jul.

The surname, area and job fields only for members from Poole. (you will need to set up a new extract range)

Activity 7. Using Database Statistical Functions

You have already used the Excel functions SUM and AVERAGE in previous activities. A function is a built-in, predefined formula; Excel provides a large number of them, some of which we will be using in future chapters.

Excel offers a number of special database functions, e.g. DSUM, DAVERAGE, DMIN, DMAX. Rather than operating on a whole range of cells as the ordinary statistical functions SUM, AVERAGE, MIN and MAX do, they can select particular records on which to operate.

For example, in the ORDERS database you can find not only the average order value, but the average order value for a particular customer, or since a certain date.

A fuller list of database functions is given at the end of this chapter.

1. Open the worksheet ORDERS.XLS – see activity 3, Figure 3.5.
   Select the cells and define them as a database, using the Data menu as before.

2. You will also need to reset the search criteria again. First remove the ones used in the previous activity.
   Copy the field names from row 1 and paste them to row 13. Select them again, plus the 7 cells underneath them, ie. cell range A13 to G14.
   Open the Data menu and select Set Criteria.

3. Taking DSUM as an example, database functions have the form,
   DSUM(database,"field",criteria)
   database is the database range that you have defined in section 1. above.
   field is the field that you wish to sum.
   criteria is the criteria range that you have defined in section 2.

4. Let's use the DSUM function to total up the VAT that Wilson Garages have to pay on their orders.
    Activate cell D17 and enter the formula:=DSUM(database,"VAT",criteria)
    Click the tick box.
    The VAT for all records is summed and placed in cell D17 as we have entered no search criterion yet.
    Error Messages. If you get an error message then check that the field name is spelt correctly and entered in double quotes.
    Check that you have placed the commas and brackets correctly.
    Notice also that there are no spaces in the formula, and that you can use upper or lower case.
    Now enter the search criterion Wilson Garages in cell D14. The VAT total will change to reflect this.

5. Amend the formula and the search criterion so that it sums the Total field for records for Marsden Products.
    The total should be £7177.53.

6. Now let's designate a section of the worksheet for several database functions.
    First clear cell formula and erase any search conditions.
    Now, starting in cell A16, enter the cell titles shown in Figure 3.12. Centre and embolden them.

	A	B	C	D	E	F
				ORDERS3.S		
9	14007	9-Mar	1453	Wilson Garages	2654.00	464.45
10	14000	10-Mar	1453	Wilson Garages	3200.44	560.08
11	14003	11-Mar	1289	Marsden Products	4456.00	779.80
12						
13	Order No.	Order Date	Co. Ref	Co. Name	Value	Vat
14						
15						
16	No. of Orders	Avg. Value	Total Value	Total Vat	Min. Total	
17						

Figure 3.12

7. In cell A17 we will use the DCOUNT function to count the number of orders; enter the formula =DCOUNT(database,"total",criteria)

8. Activate cell B17 next and use the DAVERAGE function to calculate the average value of an order.
    The formula is, DAVERAGE(database,"value",criteria)

9. **Consolidation**. Use the DSUM function to calculate cell C17 – the total value of invoices.
    Similarly calculate cell D17 – the total VAT – see section 4.

10. Cell E17 uses the DMIN function to find the order with the minimum value. Enter the formula DMIN(database,"value",criteria)

11. Using the Format menu, format the formulae cells A17 to E17 to 2 decimal places.

12. We have now created a number of formulae that use database functions and can apply them to particular records.
    Enter the Co. Ref 2413 in cell C14 as a search criterion; the values in all the formulae cells change to reflect the totals for this company's orders.
    Reading across row 17, 2 orders are counted, their average value is £1016.50, etc.

13. **Consolidation**. Every time the search criteria in row 14 are changed the formulae immediately recalculate the results. Enter the following search criteria:

    a. Order numbers 14005 onwards.

    b. Orders with VAT amounts less than £250.

    c. Orders totalling less than £1000 or more than £5000.
        (you will need to reset the criteria range to use an 'or' condition – see activity 5.10)

14. Create a further heading 'Max. Total' in cell F16.
    Use the DMAX function to create a formula in cell F17 that calculates the maximum order total.

Summary of Commands and Functions.

Note: Menu commands show the menu name first, followed by the command to choose from the menu, e.g. Edit-Clear means open the Edit menu and select the Clear command.

Commands

*	Substitute for characters in a search
?	Substitute for single character in a search
Data-Extract	Extract records matching the search criteria
Data-Find	Find records matching the search criteria
Data-Form	Use a data form
Data-Series	Create a data series
Data-Set Criteria	Define search criteria
Data-Set Database	Define selected cells as a database
Data-Sort	Sort selected cells

Database Functions

Database functions have the form, [FUNCTION](database,"field",criteria):
database is the database range that you have defined.
field is the field name or cell reference in the database on which the function operates and must be enclosed in double quotes.
criteria is the criteria range that you have defined.

DAVERAGE	Average a numeric field
DCOUNT	Count number of records
DMAX	Find maximum
DMIN	Find minimum
DPRODUCT	Multiply
DSTDEV	Calculate standard deviation
DSUM	Add
DVAR	Calculate variance

Chapter 4: Advanced Worksheet Operations

Introduction to the Chapter

This chapter extends the worksheet skills gained in Chapter 1 in several ways.
It shows you how to link several worksheets together and how to protect your worksheets from accidental alteration.
It shows you how to use Excel analysis tools to manipulate variables and solve problems.
Finally it gives you practice in using some more advanced Excel Functions.

Summary of Skills Covered

Skill	Activity	Skill	Activity
Functions – getting Help	12	Protecting cells	3.4
Goal Seek – using	7	Protecting documents	3.1
Information Window – using	13	Scenario Manager – using	11
Linking formulae	2	Solver Report – creating	9.10
Linking worksheets	1,2	Solver – using	9
Lookup tables – using	6	Two-input tables – using	5
Naming cells	4.2	What If Macro – using	8
One-Input tables – using	4	Workbooks – using	14

Activity 1. Linking Worksheets – Part 1

Excel allows you to link worksheets together, so that you can share and exchange data between them. This has a number of advantages:

a. You can edit the linked worksheets as a group; changes made to one worksheet will be reflected in the others.

b. The Excel windowing facility means that several worksheets can be open in memory at once so that you can see the results of any changes.

c. Although you could create several smaller worksheets within one large worksheet, this is not such a good idea. Apart from the security issue of accidental errors and erasure of data in a large worksheet, moving around one large worksheet can be cumbersome. Several smaller 'pages' are easier to read than one large page!

A typical linking application is the departments or branches of a company. The same type of financial or numeric data is recorded for each, and they are combined into an overall summary.

We will create a set of simple budgets for a group of three hotels – Greenlands, Whiteways, and Blueskies – and combine into an overall summary.

1. We will first create a master worksheet, copy it and then customise it for each hotel.
   Open a new worksheet.

	A	B	C	D	E
			BUDGMAS.XLS		
1			BUDGET - 1ST QUARTER		
2					
3		JAN	FEB	MAR	TOTAL
4	No. of Rooms				0
5	No. of Days	31	28	31	90
6	Occupancy Rate	0.7	0.6	0.65	
7	Av. Rate per Room	40	40	40	
8	Total Room Revenue	0	0	0	0
9	Estim. DOP - Rooms	0	0	0	0
10	Estim. Food Revenue	0	0	0	0
11	Estim. DOP food	0	0	0	0
12					
13	Total Operating Profit	0	0	0	0
14					

Figure 4.1

2. Enter the data and formulae as follows, using the data in Figure 4.1 as a guide:
   Row 4. No. of Rooms. Leave this blank as it will vary between hotels/months.
   Row 5. The number of days in the month.
   Row 6. Occupancy Rate (not every available room is let). Enter as 0.7 (i.e. 70%) for Jan, Feb etc. as shown.
   Row 7. Av. Rate per Room. This is £40, the average charged per room per day, excluding food. Do not enter a £ sign.

   Rows 4 to 7 hold all the variables, the remaining rows are all based on formulae.

   Row 8. Total Room Revenue is the product of the first 4 cells, i.e. the formula is B4*B5*B6*B7
   Enter this formula in cell B8 and fill right for Feb and Mar. It will show a value of O until row 4 is completed.
   Row 9. Estimated DOP – Rooms. The direct operating profit or DOP is estimated as 40% of Total Room Revenue – cell B8.
   Enter this formula (B8*0.4) and fill right as before.
   Row 10. The Estimated Food Revenue is 45% of the Total Room Revenue. Enter this formula and fill right.
   Row 11. The Estimated Direct Operating Profit – Food is 45% of the Estimated Food Revenue – cell B10.
   Enter this formula and fill right.

Row 13. Total Operating Profit is the operating profits for food and for rooms added together, i.e. B9+B11.
Enter this formula and fill right.

3. Create the TOTAL column by adding across the 3 months for the categories shown. (do not add the Occupancy Rate or the Rate per Room – these cannot sensibly be summed)
As a check that your formulae are correct, enter the figure 100 in cell B4.
Your Total Operating Profit should be 52,297. Erase this entry once you have checked it.

4. Finally format the cells holding the numeric data to 2 decimal places.
Save the worksheet as BUDGMAS.
You now have an empty matrix, ready to copy to create budgets for the 3 hotels.

5. Now select all the worksheet cells, i.e. A1 to E13.
Open the Edit menu and select Copy.

6. Open the File menu and select New.
A dialogue box appears, click OK to select a new worksheet.
When the new blank worksheet appears, open the Edit menu and select Paste.
You now have a copy of BUDGMAS, widen the columns if necessary.

7. Repeat step 6 twice more to produce two more copies of BUDGMAS.
You should now be able to see the overlapping edges of 4 worksheets – BUDGMAS, plus 3 copies.
If you can only see one worksheet then you probably need to use the Restore button to reduce the window size.

8. To practise moving between worksheet windows do **either** of the following:

    a. Click on the edge of a worksheet, or

    b. Use the Window menu to select the worksheet by name.

9. Each new worksheet, SHEET2, SHEET3 etc., will represent one of the three hotels – Greenlands, Whiteways, and Blueskies.
Activate each one in turn and, before you save each worksheet, enter the number of rooms for each hotel in row 4 as follows:

	Jan	Feb	Mar
GREEN	55	48	55
WHITE	72	66	75
BLUE	92	88	95

10. Then save them respectively as, GREEN, WHITE, and BLUE.
    Amend the title of each worksheet to include the name of the hotel.

11. We now need to create a 4th copy of BUDGMAS to hold an overall summary of the totals of the 3 other worksheets. This time **copy the title and cell labels only** to a new worksheet, not the data and formulae.
    Save the worksheet as SUMMARY1.

12. Now activate BUDGMAS and close it using the File menu.
    Closing worksheets that you are not using saves on the computer's internal memory.

Excel 3 13. **Excel 3**. Open the Window menu and select Arrange All.
    This gives you a 'tiled' view of all 4 worksheets side by side – see Figure 4.2.

Excel 4   **Excel 4**. Open the Window menu and select Arrange.
    Experiment with Tiled and other arrangements see Figure 4.2.

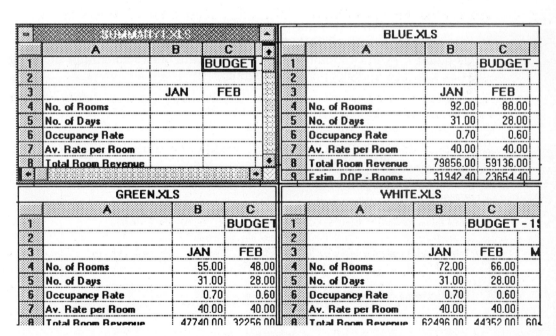

Figure 4.2

14. We have now created the four worksheets that we wish to link.

Activity 2. Linking Worksheets – Part 2

1. We can now use the worksheet SUMMARY1 to link the worksheets using external references.

   Activate SUMMARY1 and select cell B4, the No. of Rooms for January.
   We want to create a formula that adds together the contents of cell B4 for the 3 hotels and places them in cell B4 in the summary worksheet.
   Click cell B4 in the SUMMARY1 worksheet; this activates both the worksheet and the cell.

2. Type the formula =WHITE.XLS!B4+BLUE.XLS!B4+GREEN.XLS!B4 in this cell.
   This linking formula contains external references to 3 different worksheets. (each external reference must consist of the full name of the external worksheet, plus the cell reference, both separated by an exclamation mark)
   Click the tick box in the Formula Bar and the number of rooms for January at the 3 hotels is placed in cell B4 in worksheet SUMMARY1.

3. Now click the Maximise button in the SUMMARY1 worksheet.
   Select cells B4 to D4, then use Fill Right to copy the formula to cells C4 and D4.
   The linking formulae, with their external references, are copied to the 2 other cells.
   Continue to use Fill Down and Fill Right to produce summary totals for all the relevant cells in the SUMMARY1 worksheet – see Figure 4.3
   Rows 6 and 7 – the Occupancy Rate and Av. Rate per room cannot meaningfully be summed and should be left blank.

	A	B	C	D	E	F
1			BUDGET - 1ST QUARTER - SUMMARY			
2						
3		JAN	FEB	MAR	TOTAL	
4	No. of Rooms	219.00	202.00	225.00	646.00	
5	No. of Days	93.00	84.00	93.00	270.00	
6	Occupancy Rate					
7	Av. Rate per Room					
8	Total Room Revenue	190,092.00	135,744.00	181,350.00	507,186.00	
9	Estim. DOP - Rooms	76,036.80	54,297.60	72,540.00	202,874.40	
10	Estim. Food Revenue	85,541.40	61,084.80	81,607.50	228,233.70	
11	Estim. DOP food	38,493.63	27,488.16	36,723.38	102,705.17	
12						
13	Total Operating Profit	114,530.43	81,785.76	109,263.38	305,579.57	

Figure 4.3

4. Format the cells as shown to include commas; the columns may need to be widened to accommodate this new number format. (a row of hash symbols – ##### – indicates a cell that is too narrow)

5. Open the Window menu and select Arrange or Arrange All to view the 4 worksheets in tiled display again.
   Changes made to any three of the **supporting** worksheets WHITE, GREEN, or BLUE – will be reflected in the summary or **dependent** worksheet SUMMARY1.
   Try the two following 'what if' experiments:

   a. At the moment the group's Total Operating Profit for January is £114,530.43. The target is £120,000
      Amend the Av. Rate per Room for Jan.(B7) to 42 for each of the three hotels in turn.
      Does this achieve the target?

   b. The occupancy rate for March for Greenways Hotel drops to 60% (amend cell D6 on the GREEN worksheet).
      Does this allow the group to achieve the target of 125,000 Total Operating Profit for the three hotels?

6. **Saving Linked Worksheets**. All 4 linked worksheets have been named and saved.
   Exit from the 3 supporting worksheets first as follows:
   Click one of the supporting worksheets, e.g. GREEN.XLS, first to activate it.
   Open the File menu and select Close.
   You will be prompted to save the worksheet as you have changed it since the last Save. Do this.

7. Repeat these steps for the 2 other supporting worksheets.
   Finally close and save the dependent worksheet SUMMARY1.XLS.
   Make a habit of exiting in this order, if you close the dependent worksheet first there is a danger that any external formula may be lost.

8. **Opening and Using Linked Worksheets**. It is not necessary that all the linked worksheets be open for the links to operate.
   To make this point open one of the supporting worksheets, WHITE.XLS.
   Amend the Occupancy Rate for Feb. to 0.66.
   Save and Close the worksheet.

9. Now open the SUMMARY1 worksheet; a message appears, 'Update references to unopened documents ?'
   Click the Yes button and observe the totals for Feb. They are updated to reflect the changes made in the supporting worksheet, WHITE.XLS.

Activity 3. Protecting a Worksheet

Excel allows you to protect a worksheet from being opened or changed. This is vital if the document contains sensitive data or formulae which could be deleted, amended or overwritten.
Similar protection is available to charts and macro sheets, and various levels of protection are possible.

1. **Protecting an Entire Document**. Open the worksheet SUMMARY1. This worksheet uses external references in order to extract data from its three supporting worksheets, BLUE, GREEN and WHITE (see previous activities).
   Once these formulae are established they should be protected from any amendment.

2. Open the Options menu and select Protect Document.
   A dialogue box appears offering 4 options:
   Password. If you use a password it may be up to 15 characters long – numbers, letters, spaces or symbols.
   Hint. If you forget it you cannot unprotect the document; You must also remember to match the case – upper or lower – that you use.
   Cells protects cell contents from being changed.
   Objects protects any graphics objects that you may have incorporated in your worksheet from alteration e.g. lines, boxes, or embedded charts.
   Windows prevents the worksheet window being re-sized, moved or closed. Leave this option unselected.

   Click the OK button.

3. Try amending any of the worksheet cells; a message warns you that they are locked.
   To unprotect a worksheet select Unprotect Document from the Options menu.
   Close and save the SUMMARY1 worksheet.

4. **Protecting Cells**. Open the worksheet BLUE.XLS.
   Cells B4 to D7 contain numeric data that need to remain amendable.
   The data in the remaining rows are all based on formulae that need protecting from alteration. (this is standard practice, as a complex model may be destroyed by accidentally keying data into formula cells)

5. Select all the worksheet cells.(A1 to E13)
   Open the Format menu and select the option Cell Protection.

The dialogue box offers the options:

Locked. This is already selected and protects cells from alteration.

Hidden. The cell values are still displayed, but the formulae do not appear in the formula bar.
Do not select this option.

Click the OK button.

6. Open the Options menu and select the option Protect Document. Click OK.
Do not input a password. In business situations it may be useful, but if you forget it you will not be able to change your worksheet!
Try amending any of the worksheet cells. A message warns you that they are locked.

7. We now need to unprotect cell range B4 to D7. These are the 12 data entry cells that users may change. The rest are label and formula cells that must remain protected.
Open the Options menu and select Unprotect Document. Select cells B4 to D7.
Open the Format menu and choose Cell Protection.
Click the Locked box to remove the X. Click OK.
Open the Options menu again and select Protect Document. Click OK.
These data cells may now be changed. Experiment if you wish, but restore the original values.
Close and save the BLUE worksheet.

8. **Consolidation**. Repeat steps 4 to 6 above to protect the worksheets GREEN.XLS and WHITE.XLS.

9. Higher Levels of Security. Excel allows more stringent security levels, which we will review but not use.
Open the worksheet SUMMARY1.
Open the File menu and select Save as.
When the dialogue box appears click the Options button. Three types of security are offered:

Protection Password. Entering a password in this box prevents the document from being opened unless the password is entered first.

Write Reservation. Entering a password in this box prevents any changes to the documents being made unless you know the password. If you do not know it the changed document must be saved as a new document under a new name.

This is useful for protecting template documents, e.g. BUDGMAS, from being overwritten.

Read-Only Recommended. Selecting this box will prompt (but not compel) users to open the worksheet as read-only. This alerts users if a document should not be changed unless necessary.

Activity 4. One-input Tables

We have seen in previous activities how we can perform 'what if' analysis by substituting different values in formulae.

If we want to test a range of values it is quicker to use a data table rather than change them one by one.

1. **One-input tables**. We will set up a one-input table first, which sets up a range of values for one variable. Create the worksheet shown in Figure 4.4 as follows:

	A	B	C
1		Mortgage Repayments Schedule	
2			
3	Interest Rate	10%	
4	Repayment Term	240	(enter term in months)
5	Amount Borrowed	50000	
6			
7	Possible Interest	Repayment p.m.	
8	Rates		
9	9.00%		
10	9.25%		
11	9.50%		
12	9.75%		
13	10.00%		
14	10.25%		
15	10.50%		
16	10.75%		
17	11.00%		
18			

Figure 4.4

Centre and embolden the title and cell labels as shown.

Use a data series to produce the range of percentages in column C. (consult Chapter 3, Activity 1 if necessary) Enter 9.00% in cell A9; the Step value is 0.25% and the Stop Value is 11.00%.

Enter the interest rate as 10% in cell B3 – the percentage sign must be entered.

Enter the repayment term as 240 in cell B4.
(240 months = 20 years)
Enter the amount borrowed as 50000 in cell B5.
Format cells B4 and B5 to number format 0.00.
Use the Border option on the Format menu to outline cell B8, where the result will appear.
Save the worksheet as MORTGAGE.

2. **Naming Cells**. Instead of referring to cells by their row and column references, we can name them and use their names in formulae and functions.
   Names can be shorter and easier to remember than cell references.
   Select cell B3, then open the Formula menu and select Define Name. A dialogue box appears.
   Enter the name RATE, then click OK.
   Similarly name cell B4 TERM, and cell B5 AMOUNT.
   We will use these cell names in the formula that follows.

3. We will use the PMT function to calculate the monthly repayments.
   The Help facility (press F1) will tell you more about this function; it is used to calculate payments such as mortgages made at regular intervals, at fixed interest rates.
   The format is, =PMT(interest,term,principal) where interest is the interest rate, term is the repayment term, and principal the amount borrowed.
   Select cell B8 and enter the formula; =PMT(rate/12,term,-amount)
   The monthly repayment of 482.52 is entered in cell B8, based on the values entered in cell B3 to B5.
   If not check the cell data and the formula.

4. To find out the effect on the monthly repayments if the mortgage interest rate changes, we need to define the table, using the interest rates in cells A9-A17.
   Select cell range A8 to B17.
   Open the Data menu and select the Table option; a dialogue box appears.
   Select the Column Input Cell box and enter the cell reference B3. Click OK.

5. The table of monthly repayments for different rates of interest is shown in cells B9 to B17, allowing 'what if' comparisons with the repayment shown in cell B8.
   Format the table entries to 2 decimal places.

   Consolidation. Amend the interest rate to 9%, and the amount borrowed to 70000.
   You should be repaying 629.81 per month. At what interest rate would you start to pay more than £700 per month?

6. **Adding Further Formulae to the One-input table**. We can create another table, showing the effect of changing interest rates on another variable – see Figure 4.5.

   Let's show the total cost of the loan; this is the product of the monthly repayment and the term of the loan.

   Put the title Total Repaid in cell C7.

   Enter the formula =B8*TERM in cell C8. Format to two decimal places.

   Now select the cell range A8 to C17 (the new table range) Open the Data menu and select the Table option.

   Select the Column Input Cell box and enter the cell reference B3. Click OK.

   Format the table values to number format #,##0.00 and centre.

   The worksheet will now resemble Figure 4.5.

   You have created a second table in column C, showing the total amount repaid over the period of the loan

	A	B	C
1		Mortgage Repayments Schedule	
2			
3	Interest Rate	0.10	
4	Repayment Term	240.00	(enter term in months)
5	Amount Borrowed	35000.00	
6			
7	Possible Interest	Repayment p.m.	Total Repaid
8	Rates	337.76	81,061.82
9	9.00%	314.90	75,576.98
10	9.25%	320.55	76,932.81
11	9.50%	326.25	78,299.02
12	9.75%	331.98	79,675.42
13	10.00%	337.76	81,061.82
14	10.25%	343.58	82,458.04
15	10.50%	349.43	83,863.91
16	10.75%	355.33	85,279.23
17	11.00%	361.27	86,703.82

Figure 4.5

7. **Consolidation**. Alter the interest rate to 10.5%, the term to 360, and the amount borrowed to 65,000.

   a. What is the total amount repaid?

   b. What are the monthly repayments?

Activity 5. Two-input Tables

The one-input data table that you have just used is one-dimensional; it consists of one column and can only show values based on one variable – the interest rate.

We built a second table to show the total amount repaid. This was based on another formula, but still based on the same variable.

In this activity we will use a two-input table to calculate salesperson's monthly commission – see Figure 4.6 below.

	A	B	C	D	E	F
		MONTHLY COMMISSION TABLE				
1						
2						
3			Commission Rate			
4						
5		0	5%	6%	7%	8%
6		50,000	2500	3000	3500	4000
7		60,000	3000	3600	4200	4800
8	Monthly Sales	70,000	3500	4200	4900	5600
9		80,000	4000	4800	5600	6400
10		90,000	4500	5400	6300	7200
11						
12	*Enter No. of Months :-*	1				

Figure 4.6

It uses a two-dimensional table or matrix; one variable, monthly sales, is in column B, the other, the commission rate, is in rows C to F.

1. Start a new worksheet and enter the title and cell labels as shown.
   If you wish use the data series command to create the row of percentages and the column of different sales figures.
   Don't enter anything in row 12 yet.

2. The commission earned is the commission rate multiplied by the monthly sales.
   The formula must be entered where the row and column variables intersect.
   Select cell B5 and enter the formula =B3*B4
   You may wonder why cells B3 and B4 have been chosen.
   In fact we won't be entering values in these cells. This is because in this example the two-input table provides the full range of values we are interested in. (unlike the previous example of the one-input table – see figure 4.4)

However the table needs to use two cells when it calculates its values. We nominated B3 and B4, but could use any empty cell outside the table.

3. Now select the table, i.e. cell range B5 to F10.
   Open the Data menu and select Table.
   Enter B3 as the row input cell and B4 as the column input cell.
   The commission table is calculated, equivalent to 25 separate calculations (see Figure 4.6). This makes the table a valuable tool.
   Save the worksheet as COMMISS.XLS.

4. **Consolidation**. We will adapt the table so that we can calculate the commission for a number of months.
   Enter the label in cell A12 – see Figure 4.6. above. Now format cell B12 with a double border as shown.
   Amend the table formula in cell B5 to include cell B12 in its product
   Now enter 6 in cell B12.
   The table is recalculated, showing the commission earned for 6 months.

5. **More Information on tables.**

   Move or delete a table. Select the whole table and then select Cut or Clear from the Edit menu.

   Modify a table. Select the whole table and choose the Table command from the Data menu.

   Extend the range of a table. Enter the extra values then proceed as for modify.

Activity 6 Lookup Tables

The table values in the previous activities were generated using variables and a formula.
The user input a number of variables, e.g. mortgage amount, term, etc. and a formula; then the Table command built a table based around one or more of these variables
A lookup table involves the reverse procedure; the table is already created and you need to look up a value in it.
Look at Figure 4.7

	A	B	C	D	E	F
1				Order Discount		
2						
3	*Cash Order*					
4	Order Value					
5	Discount					
6	Net value			Order Value	Cash	Credit
7				0	5%	0%
8	*Credit Order*			500	10%	5%
9	Order Value			1000	15%	10%
10	Discount			5000	20%	15%
11	Net value			10000	25%	20%
12						

Figure 4.7

On the right of the worksheet is a table to look up customer discounts, based on the value of the order – from 0 to 10000 – and type of order – cash or credit. As the discount rates in the table do not follow any obvious numeric sequence, using a formula to generate them would be difficult.

You can use two lookup functions to get data from a table, HLOOKUP and VLOOKUP:

HLOOKUP is used if the lookup values are arranged horizontally in a row.

The syntax is: HLOOKUP(x,range,index)

VLOOKUP is used if the lookup values are arranged vertically in a column, as they are in the discount table (the more usual arrangement).

The syntax is: VLOOKUP(x,range,index)

x is the value in the first column or row of the table that you are looking up; it can be text, a number or a cell reference.

range is the range of cells forming the table.

Index tells you which column or row to look in.

Lookup tables can be used for various types of fixed information that can be accessed by another part of the worksheet, e.g. rates of pay, credit ratings or addresses.

The first column of the lookup table consists of entries that are used to look up items of data immediately adjacent columns, as in Figure 4.7.

These entries must be unique and in ascending order.

1. Create the data shown in figure 4.7. and enter an order value of 600 in cell B4.

2. In cell B5 enter the formula =VLOOKUP(B4,D7:F11,2)
   This means 'look up the value in cell B4, from the table cell range D7 to F11, in the 2nd column'.
   The lookup function searches the first column of compare values until it reaches a number equal to or higher than 600, goes back a row if it is higher, then goes to the second column and looks up the discount of 10% (in cell E8)

For this reason the values in the first column of the lookup table – column D – must be in ascending sequence.

3. The formula to calculate the net value of the order (order value minus discount) can now be entered in cell B6.
    Enter the formula = B4-(B4*B5) in this cell.

4. Now repeat these steps to calculate the discount on credit orders.
    You will need to adjust the cell references in the second VLOOKUP formula.

5. Save the worksheet as DISCT1.

Activity 7. Analysis Tools 1 – Goal Seek

The 'what-if?' abilities of Excel allow us to try out many alternatives for a given situation.
In previous activities we have used input and lookup tables to compare values for one or more variables.
In the next few activities we will look at special-purpose analysis tools.
The first and simplest is Goal Seek; often you want to know what value a variable needs to be for a formula to equal a particular value. Goal Seek keeps changing the value of the variable until the formula achieves the target value.

1. Open the worksheet BLUE.XLS. You will recall from Activity 1 that it calculates the quarterly operating profit for Blueskies Hotel.
    We want to find out what occupancy rate for February would achieve a total operating profit of £40,000 for this month. We could keep amending the occupancy rate cell C6 and observe the effects, but Goal Seek is easier.

2. Open the Formula menu and select Goal Seek.
    A dialogue box appears; if necessary move the box so that you can see column C. (position the screen pointer on the title of the box, and drag it using the mouse)

3. Complete the box as follows:
    Set cell   C13
    To value   40000
    By changing cell C6

    Make a note of the present value of cell C6 and click OK. A further dialogue box appears reporting the solution 40,000.
    The value of cell C6 is changed to 0.67 – the occupancy rate needed to reach the £40,000 goal.

4. Click the Cancel button now; this restores the previous value for cell C7 and all the dependent cells.
    If you click OK by accident then select Undo from the Edit menu.

5. Now try the following Goal Seek; what average rate per room for January would achieve a total room revenue of £100,000 for that month?

6. **Consolidation.** Open the worksheet TERM1.XLS. and scroll to week 9. How large a loan would you need in week 9 to achieve a closing balance of £150?

7. Close the worksheets BLUE and TERM1 without saving any changes.

8. **More about Goal Seek.**
    The dialogue box displays two extra buttons;

    Pause – allows you to pause during goal seeking
    Step – allows you to continue one step at a time.

    Goal seeking will only work if the cell whose value you set contains a value, not a formula.
    The cell whose value you set must be related by a formula to the cell whose target value you are changing.

Activity 8. Analysis Tools 2 – The What If Macro

If you want to change the value of more than one variable you should use Excel's What If macro rather than Goal Seek. It allows you to define as many values as you want for each variable and then cycle through each combination one by one. This is much easier than doing it manually; for example if you assign 3 values each to 2 variables there are 9 possible combinations of values. Assigning a range of 4 values to 3 variables would give 64 combinations.

1. First load the worksheet WHITE.XLS and maximise the window. The occupancy rate for the hotel and the number of days that it is open may vary in January. We will test the effect of various values on revenue and profit.

2. Before you can use the What If macro you must install it on your menu.
    Open the File menu and select Open.
    The Open menu may confirm that you are already using the Excel directory on C drive. If so, miss out the first two steps of the following instructions and go to step c.

Excel 3

Excel 3 only
  a. Double click on C\: in the Directories list – a new list opens.

Excel 4

Excel 4 only
  a. Move the screen pointer to the Drives box and click the down arrow symbol.
      A list of drives appears; select the C: icon then OK.

All Excel versions

All Excel Versions
  b. Double click on Excel in the Directories list. The contents of the Excel directory are shown in the Directories list.

  c. Double click on the Library directory.

  d. Scroll to the bottom of the Files box if necessary and select the file WHATIF.XLA

3. The What If macro is now loaded and you are returned to the worksheet. (the first time that you use the What If macro during an Excel session you must load it in this way)

4. Open the Formula menu and choose What If – if the option is missing or does not work then repeat step 2 above.
    A dialogue box appears.
    Click the New button to select a new data sheet. This sheet will hold the range of values for each variable.
    We are now ready to enter a range of values for cell B5. This holds the days of the month and may vary from 29-31, depending on the number of days the hotel is open.

5. A further What If box appears now – 'Reference of Variable #1'.
    Enter B5 and click OK.

6. **Entering Values for Variables**. The dialogue box changes again, prompting you for the first value for B5.
    Enter 29 and click OK.
    You are now prompted for the 'Value #2 for B5'.
    Enter 30 and click OK.
    Finally enter 31 in the 'Value #3 for B5' box.
    This time click OK then the Done button.

7. You are now prompted to supply the cell reference of the second variable. We want to vary the occupancy rate, so enter the cell reference B6 and click OK.

8. Repeat step 6 to enter the values 0.7, 0.75 and 0.8.
    When you enter the final value click select the OK then the Done button; you are prompted for a third variable.
    Click Done again to stop at 2 variables.
    Now that we have set up the values for the variables we can cycle through them, either one at a time or both at once.

9. **Substituting one variable at a time**. Select cell B5 that holds the first variable.
    Hold down the Ctrl key and press the letter t key once the first value is substituted.
    Repeat this and the three values for the variable are substituted. you can observe the effect that this has on revenue and profits.
    Repeat this to display the next range of variables in cell B6.

10. **Substituting for all variables at once**. Hold down the Shift and Ctrl keys and press the t key.
    You can cycle through all 9 combinations
    Work out the answers to the following questions.
    Which combination of values gives you a total operating profit:

    a. for January closest to £42,400?

    b. for the quarter closest to £80,000?

11. **Finishing and saving**. After cycling through the various combinations of values you could decide to keep some preferred combination or revert to the original ones.
    We will keep the originals (i.e. No of Days = 31 and Occupancy Rate = 0.7) to avoid affecting the linked worksheet SUMMARY – see Activity 2.
    Either cycle back to the original values or re-key them. Closing the worksheet without saving it would have the same effect.
    Use the Window menu to view the data sheet, it has the temporary name Sheet1 or Sheet2 etc.
    We could save the data sheet if we wished to use it again with the What If macro.
    Close the data sheet(s) without saving, then close the worksheet WHITE.

Activity 9. Analysis tools – Solver

The What If macro used in the previous activity can substitute various values for variables in a formula.

It will not of itself determine what the 'best' ones are for your purpose.

Solver, as its name suggests, can solve certain types of problem. It will juggle with multiple values for variables and find the combination producing the optimum or target result, e.g. it can determine the most profitable mix of products, schedule staff to minimise the wages bill, or allocate working capital to its most profitable use.

Solver allows you to specify up to two hundred variables; it also allows you to put constraints on variables by specifying the limits that they can take e.g. minimum and maximum values for a machine's output or for a working week.

Solver is an Excel's most powerful analysis tool and uses a fairly complex mathematical method to solve equations and arrive at its optimum or target values.

It tries out various input values for the formulae and observes, not only the corresponding outputs, but also their rate of change. Each trial is known as an iteration.

The results of a previous iteration is analyzed and used to work out the next set of trial inputs. Solver converges on the optimum or target value by repeated trials or iterations. This method is much quicker than Goal Seek, What If or manual calculations, especially if you are working with multiple variables and constraints.

However Solver poses certain problems for the user:

a. There are a fairly limited range of problems that can or need to be solved in this way.

b. For complex problems there may be more than one solution; Solver may provide the best given the range of values that you have specified, but it may not be the best overall. You may need to run Solver more than once with different ranges of values.

c. To use Solver effectively then you must thoroughly understand the nature of the problem that you are trying to solve, otherwise Solver will either fail to work altogether or give you misleading results.

We will first set up a typical Solver problem – see Figure 4.8.

	A	B	C	D	E	F	G	H	I	J
1		Staff Scheduling - New Branch.								
2										
3	Rota	Rest Days :-	Employees		Mon	Tue	Wed	Thu	Fri	Sat
4			Per Rota							
5	1	Mon, Tues			0	0	1	1	1	1
6	2	Tues, Wed.			1	0	0	1	1	1
7	3	Wed., Thurs			1	1	0	0	1	1
8	4	Thurs, Fri			1	1	1	0	0	1
9	5	Fri, Sat			1	1	1	1	0	0
10			0							
11		Staff Allocated per day :-			0					
12										
13		Staff Needed per Day :-			14	14	16	17	20	22
14										
15		Ave. pay per day (£) :-	30							
16		Wages Bill for Week :-	0							

Figure 4.8

Your company wishes to open a new branch and needs to work out the optimum staff loading throughout the working week of Monday to Saturday.

The number of staff needed each day has been estimated in row 13; more staff are needed towards the weekend as the branch gets busier.

Each staff member gets 2 consecutive rest days; these are staggered to produce 5 different rotas – see columns A and B.

In columns E to J this is represented as a 0 for a rest day and 1 for a working day.

You need to work out:

a. How many staff need to be on each rota (cells C5-C9)

b. To ensure that the staff allocated each day (cells E11-J11), covers the number of staff needed (cells E13-J13)

A problem will be that to achieve full staffing levels on busy days means that on other days we may need to employ more staff then we need.

1. First let's build the basic worksheet; start a new worksheet and create the title and cell labels. Then enter the figures shown.
   Format cell ranges C5 to C9 and E11 to J11 as whole numbers. All staff are full time so no fractional amounts are allowed.

2. Apply the following formulae:

   a. Cell C10 is the sum of cells C5 to C9.

   b. Cell C16 is the product of cells C10 and C15.

c. For each of the 5 rotas you need to multiply column C – the number of staff working the rota – by column E which indicates whether that rota is working on that day.
Enter the following formula in cell E11:
=($C5*E5)+($C6*E6)+($C7*E7)+($C8*E8)+($C9*E9)
Use the Fill Right command to copy this formula to cells F11 to J11.
The $ sign in the formula ensures that column C is an absolute reference and is copied unchanged into the new formula. Absolute references are explained more fully in Chapter 1, Activity 15.
Column E is a relative reference and gets changed when the formula is copied to row F,G,H etc.

3. Open the Formula menu and select Solver.
The Solver Parameters dialogue box appears – see Figure 4.9.

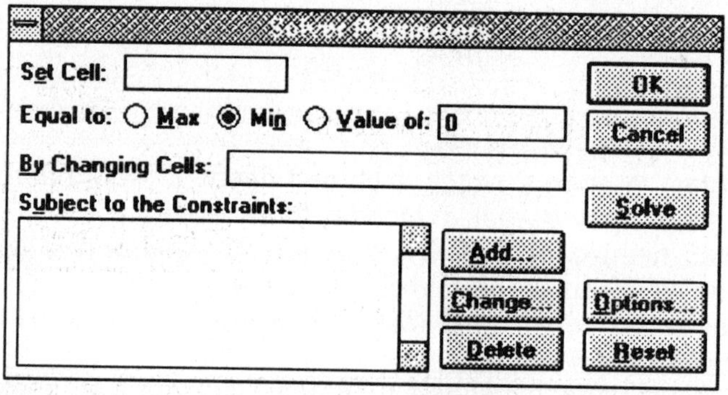

Figure 4.9

We wish to minimise the wages bill; complete the first part of the dialogue box as follows:
Set Cell box: Enter C16
Equal to buttons: Leave Min selected and 'Value of' Set to 0.

4. The cells whose values we want to vary to achieve the result are those containing the number of employees per rota.
Click the By Changing Cells box and enter C5:C9

5. We must apply two constraints now;

a. the number of staff per day must be >0 (i.e. not a negative number), and,

b. the number of staff allocated on any day must meet the demand.

Click the Add button and a new dialogue box appears – Add Constraint.
Insert the cell references C5:C9 in the cell reference box.
Change the relationship to >= in the adjacent box. Finally click the constraint box and insert 0.

Click OK and you are returned to the Solver Parameters dialogue box. The constraint is shown – $C$5:$C$9>0.
Solver converts the cell references to absolute references.
If you have made an error then click either the Change button to Edit it, or the Delete button.

6. Add the second constraint in the same way – see 5b above.
   The constraint is E11:J11>=E13:J13
   You have now finished your Solver parameters.
   The completed dialogue box should resemble Figure 4.10

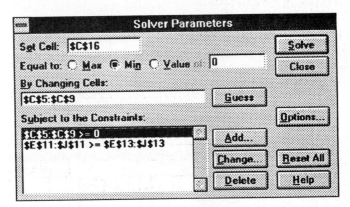

Figure 4.10

7. Click the Solve button and Solver goes through a complex series of iterations until it finds the first valid solution.
   A dialogue box appears; move this aside so that you can see the solution. Solver has worked out,

   a. how many staff need to be on each rota (cells C5 to C9) in order to ensure,

   b. that the staff allocated (cells E11 to J11) cover,

   c. the numbers of staff needed (cells E13 to J13)

   You will notice that for one day – Monday – you areoverstaffed by 3 people.

8. The Solver dialogue box offers you the option of keeping the Solver solution or restoring the original values. Click the Restore Original Values option then click OK.

9. **Consolidation.**

Call up Solver again and add a third constraint – that the staff allocated for Monday should not exceed those needed. The constraint is therefore that E11<=14
Enter this and run Solver again – you will notice that the overstaffing has merely been transferred to another part of the week.
Given the staffing needs at this branch and the rota system there is no way round this.

10. **Solver Reports**. If the Solver successful completion message box is still on the screen you may wish to generate a Solver report at this stage.
Click the Answer box then click OK. The report is generated and stored as a separate worksheet. If necessary use the Window menu to view it. It summarises all the Solver input data:
- ❏ the value of the target cell C16
- ❏ The values reached for the adjustable cells C5:C9
- ❏ How well the constraint were met – Binding means that the cell value equals the constraint value, Not Binding means that the constraint was met but the values were not equal, Not Satisfied means that the constraint value was not reached.

Save this report worksheet as SCHEDREP. Save the worksheet itself as SCHEDULE.

Activity 10. Consolidation of the Three Analysis Tools

To reinforce the three previous activities we will use Goal Seek, What If and Solver on a new example.
Create the simple worksheet shown in Figure 4.11. It shows the profits that a company makes from three products A B and C.
Format all the numbers to whole numbers.

Total columns B and C as shown, and save the worksheet as PROFIT.XLS.

	A	B	C	D	E
1					
2		No of	Profit per	Profit	
3		Units	Unit		
4					
5	Product A	100	46	4600	
6	Product B	100	53	5300	
7	Product C	100	69	6900	
8		300		16800	
9					

Figure 4.11

1. **Goal Seek**. (Refer back to Activity 7 for guidance if necessary.)
   Find out how many of product B we need to make to raise profits from £16,800 to £20,000.
   Appendix 7 shows the correct entries for the Goal Seek dialogue box.
   Do not save the Goal Seek solution.

2. **What If**. (Refer back to Activity 8 for guidance if necessary).
   If you have started a new Excel session then Instal the What If macro first, then open the Formula menu and select What If.
   We want to vary the profit per unit for Product A (cell C5).
   Enter the three values 40, 50 and 60.
   Similarly enter three different profit figures for Product C – 65, 70 and 75.
   Now cycle through the combinations of values for these variables – there are nine in all.
   The maximum and minimum profits should be £15,800 and £18,800. Check and see.
   Restore the original cell values to 46 and 69.

Excel 4   **Excel 4 Users only**. Do Activity 11 next – Scenario Manager – and then come back to the Solver Problem.

3. **Solver**. We wish to make a combined profit of £20,000 for the three products subject to the following three constraints, which are based on production capacity and customer demand:
   The maximum number we can make of Product A is 50.
   We must make at least 40 each of Products B and C.
   Overall production can rise to a maximum of 350.
   Enter these constraints into Solver and run it.
   Refer back to Activity 9 if necessary.
   Appendix 8 shows the correct Solver parameters to enter. Keep the Solver solution and quit the worksheet.

Activity 11. Excel 4 Users Only. Scenario Manager

> Scenario Manager allows you to save different combinations of variables as named scenarios to run or print them later.

1. Keep pressing the Shift-Ctrl-t keys until the minimum profits for each product are shown – 40 for Product A and 65 for Product C.

2. Open the Formula menu and select Scenario Manager.
   A dialogue box appears.
   Erase any cell references already in the box.

Hold down the Ctrl key and select cell C5 then cell C7. These are the 'Changing Cells'
Now release the Ctrl key and click the Add button.

3. The 'Add Scenario' dialogue box appears next.
Name this scenario Minimum Profit and click OK.
This scenario is stored as part of the worksheet and the Scenario Manager main dialogue box appears again.

4. Click the Add button and a second Add Scenario dialogue box appears.
Name this scenario Maximum Profit.
Enter the values 60 for cell C5 and 75 for cell C7.
Click Add.
When the third Add Scenario box appears click Cancel. The Scenario Manager dialogue box appears now.
Click Close.

5. **Running a Scenario**. Open the Formula menu and select Scenario Manager. Select the Maximum Profit scenario and click Show.
The maximum values are assigned to cells C5 and C7. Close the Scenario Manager dialogue box – the values remain assigned to the cells.

6. **Printing a Scenario**. Open the File menu and select Print Report.
The Print Report dialogue box appears – click the Add button.
The Add Report dialogue box appears.
Enter the Report Name as Min_Prof
Move the screen pointer to the Report section.
Click the down arrow on the Scenario box.
Select the scenario Minimum Profit.
Click the Add button, then the OK button.
The Print Report dialogue box appears now – check your printer.
Click the Print button and the report will print.
Now return to the previous activity, section 3.

Activity 12. More Excel Functions

Notes on Functions

❑ Functions are ready-made formulae that perform useful calculations.
❑ They produce their result in the cell in which they are entered.
❑ Every function must start with the = symbol
❑ Normally a function contains no spaces
❑ Functions can form part of a formula – or another function
❑ Functions require you to supply information for their operations. These are called arguments.

e.g SUM(range) requires the cell range to be added. Arguments must be enclosed in brackets, optional arguments are shown in the lists that follow in square brackets – [ ] These square brackets are for your guidance only and should **not** be typed.

❏ Two or more arguments are separated by commas. The commas **must** be typed.

❏ You can either type the function yourself (in upper or lower case) or open the Formula menu and select Paste Function. You can then choose the function from the list presented and paste it into the active cell.

Types of Functions

Depending on your version of Excel you can use up to 10 categories of functions:

Database Functions carry out operations on database records only, e.g. summing or averaging certain records, see chapter 3. Some are listed in the next section.

Date and time Functions are mentioned in the next section

Engineering Functions are not used in this book.

Financial Functions are discussed in the next section.

Information Functions test and report on cell references and contents; a few are listed at the end of this chapter and at the end of Chapter 6.

Logical Functions test for the truth of certain conditions. A few are listed in the next section.

Lookup Functions were discussed in Activity 6.

Mathematical and Trigonometric Functions calculate square roots, cosines etc. as well as the simpler functions such as SUM.

Statistical Functions such as average and standard deviation are dealt with later in this section.
Some are listed also in the next section.

Text Functions manipulate strings of text, e.g. finding the length or converting to upper case.
A few are listed at the end of this chapter.

It is beyond the scope of this book to deal with all of the Excel functions; many, such as trigonometric and engineering functions, have little general business application.

To use others, such as financial functions, you need some specialist background in the subject to understand the significance of the results.

Some functions we have already used, such as some of the simpler maths function in Chapter 1, and the database functions in Chapter 3.

The following activity starts lists a few widely-used functions, and is followed by example worksheets.

Other useful functions are listed at the end of this chapter.

Macro functions can only be used on macro sheets and are dealt with in Chapters 5 and 6.

Help on Functions

If you want to review the functions available in your version of Excel then use Help as follows:

a. Press the F1 Help key.

b. Click the Search button on the Help menu.

c. Type the words Worksheet Functions.

Excel 3   d. **Excel 3**. Click the Search button again.

Excel 4   d. **Excel 4**. Click the Show Topics button.

e. Select a topic , and click the Go to button.

f. Scroll through the list of functions.

g. To find out more about a particular function move the screen pointer onto the function name and click.

h. To return to the Search menu click the search button.

Date and Time Functions

Date and time functions use a serial number to calculate e.g the time elapsed between two dates or times.

Often this serial number needs formatting to produce a readable date display, e.g.

NOW() displays current date and time (see Section 2 below).

Financial Functions

Financial functions calculate such things as investments, repayments and depreciation.
It is essential that the term of investment, repayment etc. is in the same time units as the interest rate. e.g. if you are,investing £5000 over 6 months at an annual interest rate of 10%, then the interest rate must be converted to a monthly rate too.

FV(interest,payments,amount[pv,type])
Gives the future value of an investment based on a fixed interest rate, the number of payments and the amount of the payment. The payments are assumed to be equal throughout.
Options are to enter present value and whether payment is made at the end of the period (type=0, the default) or at the beginning (type=1)

NPV(interest,range)
Gives the net present value of an investment based on a fixed interest rate and series of cash flows within a given range.

PMT(interest,term,principal,[,fv,type])
Gives the repayments required for a loan amount (principal) based on the interest rate and the term.
Options are to enter future value and whether payment is made at the end of the period (type=0, the default) or at the beginning (type=1)
We have already used PMT() in Activity 4.

SLN(cost,salvage,life)
Calculates the depreciation of an asset using the straight-line method, based on the initial cost, its salvage value at the end of its life and the time period over which it is depreciated.

Statistical Functions and Database Functions

AVERAGE(range)
Gives the average value of a range of cells

MIN(range)
Gives the minimum value in a range of cells

MAX(range)
Gives the maximum value in a range of cells

STDEV(range)
Gives the standard deviation of a range of cells – how much they vary from the average

DAVERAGE, DMIN, DMAX, DSTDEV and DSUM are special database functions; they work in the same way as their statistical equivalents but can be used with search criteria – see Chapter 3, Activity 7.

Logical Functions

IF(condition,true result,false result)
Tests a condition to see if true or false, takes one action for a true result, another for a false result.

AND(condition1,condition2,....)
Tests for all conditions being true and returns a logical True

OR(condition1,condition2,.....)
tests for at least one condition being true and returns a logical True

1. We will now use some of these functions in the following worksheet, Figure 4.12.

	A	B	C	D	E	F
1		Share Analysis			2-Mar-93	
2	Date	Alpha	Beta	Gamma	Changes	Share
3		Tours	Holidays	Cruises	in Value	Performance
4	1-Sep	19.435	50.876	123.543	193.854	
5	2-Sep	19.435	51.321	122.876		
6	3-Sep	20.654	51.362	124.554		
7	4-Sep	20.304	52.000	125.562		
8	5-Sep	19.250	52.643	125.953		
9	8-Sep	21.000	53.244	125.238		
10	9-Sep	21.345	54.254	124.528		
11	10-Sep	21.465	55.340	123.865		
12	11-Sep	20.832	55.000	127.276		
13	12-Sep	20.500	53.888	124.552	198.940	share increase
14						
15	Hi Val	21.465	55.340	127.276		
16	Lo Val	19.250	50.876	122.876		
17	Av Val	20.422	52.993	124.795		
18	St Dev	0.805	1.600	1.273		

Figure 4.12

This worksheet monitors the performance of the shares of three travel companies over a two week period.
You should be able to enter most of the worksheet for yourself. I shall concentrate on the functions.

2. First we will insert the date function in cell E1; enter the formula =NOW()
   A date serial number appears.
   Format it to d-mmm-yy using the Format menu.

3. Rows 15 to 17 contain respectively the maximum, minimum and average
   value of the shares over the two weeks.
   Row 18 shows the standard deviation – the extent to which share prices
   have fluctuated from the average
   In cell B15 enter the function =MAX(B4:B13)
   In cell B16 enter the function =MIN(B4:B13)

4. Similarly apply the AVERAGE function to cell B17.
   Apply the STDEV function to cell B18.

5. Use Fill Right on the Edit menu to copy these functions to columns C and D.

6. Finally columns E and F are used to calculate how the three sets of shares
   have changed in value over the two weeks.
   Add the share values across for the three companies on the 1-Sep and 12-
   Sep as shown in Figure 4.12.

Their combined value has grown between these two dates.

7. You will see that in cell F13 a share increase is reported
   This message is produced by the logical function IF(). If the share values
   increase then this message is displayed, if not a 'share decrease' message is
   displayed.
   Activate cell F13 and enter the formula:
   =IF(E13>E4,"share increase","share decrease")
   Test the function by amending the value of cell B13 to 14.500.
   The message in cell F15 will change as the IF condition becomes false.

8. Save the worksheet as SHARES.XLS and exit.

9. **Consolidation**. Now open a new blank worksheet and try out the following
   financial functions:

   Future Value. You are going to save £1000 a year at 10% interest for 5
   years.
   Enter the following in a blank cell; =FV(10%,5,1000)
   The result is the value of your investment after 5 years. (you may need to
   widen the column to show the result.)

   Straight Line Depreciation. You have bought a PC for £1000 and esti-
   mate that in 4 years it will be worth £300. Enter the following in a blank
   cell; =SLN(1000,300,4) The result is the annual amount of depreciation.

Close the worksheet without saving.

Activity 13. Checking Your Worksheet

The worksheets that we have created have been fairly small, occupying no more than a couple of screens.

As worksheets get larger and more complex there is a danger of design and data entry errors creeping in which can invalidate the whole model. These are surprisingly common in business.

Excel has a number of tools to help you check your worksheet, some of which we have already used, e.g.:

Naming Cells. Naming cells and groups of cells make them easier to refer to and the worksheet more readable – see Activity 4.

Worksheet Protection prevents crucial data and formulae being overwritten or deleted.

View Document. The Print Preview option allows you to get an overview of the whole document – see Chapter 1, Activity 9.

In this activity we will look at the Excel Information Window facility. It allows you to get detailed information about individual cells.

1. Open the worksheet BLUE.XLS. You will remember that it is one of three linked worksheets and that some of its cells have been protected from alteration – see Activities 1 – 3.

2. Select cell B13 which shows the Total Operating Profit for January.

Excel 3   **Excel 3**. Open the Window menu and choose Show Info.

Excel 4   **Excel 4**. Open the Options menu and choose the Workspace command. Click the Information Window button then the OK button.

An Information window appears, giving the cell reference and formula.
A new set of menus appear at the top of the screen; Open the Info menu and select the following options in turn:

Value – the cell's value (unformatted) is displayed

Format – all formatting is shown, including number (0.00)

Protection – the cell's locked status is confirmed

Note – displays any notes added to the cell – this is already selected

Names – displays any named areas that include this cell

Precedents – lists any cells used by the formula in this cell (B9 and B11)

Dependents – lists any cells that use this cell in their formulas (E13)

3. The Information window should now look like Figure 4.13

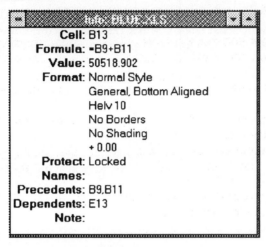

Figure 4.13

4. Not all of the information categories apply to this cell so they can be removed.
    Open the Info menu; all the options selected are 'ticked' at the moment.
    Select the Note option and it disappears from the Information window.

5. **Printing the cell information window**. Open the File menu and select Print. The information will be printed.
    Close the Information window – open the File menu and select Close. You are returned to the worksheet.
    Finally close the BLUE.XLS worksheet without saving.

6. **Searching for Cells with Specific Contents**. It is also possible to select all the cells that have particular contents. (this can be useful for spotting errors in the model)
    Open the worksheet BUDGMAS.XLS. This is the template model for all three hotels in the group – see Activities 1 and 2.
    Let's check which cells contain formulas and which contain constants, ie. data or labels.

7. Open the Formula menu and choose Select Special.
    A dialogue box appears.
    Click the Formulas button then OK. All the formulas are selected.
    Repeat this operation, this time clicking the Constants button in the dialogue box. The constants are selected.

8. We can also select all the precedents and dependents for a particular cell.
   Select cell B8.
   Choose Select Special from the Formula menu again.
   Click the Precedents button, then OK.
   The 4 cells upon which the formula in cell B8 depends are shown.

9. Now click cell B9 and choose Select Special from the Formula menu.
   Click the Dependents, then the All Levels button. Click OK.
   All the cells which use this cell, either directly (B13) or indirectly (E13) are
   selected.
   Close the BUDGMAS worksheet.

Activity 14. Excel 4 Only – Creating a Workbook

Excel 4 allows you to keep related documents together by means of a workbook. They
can be loaded in one operation, and can be viewed and worked on in one window.
Special buttons allow you to move easily between the different documents in the workbook.
Workbook documents can also be saved in one operation.
A document can appear in more than one workbook and can still be opened as a single
document if desired.

1. Close all files that are open at the moment.

2. Open the five related worksheets BUDGMAS, SUMMARY1, BLUE, GREEN
   and WHITE.

3. Open the Window menu and Select Arrange.
   Choose the Tiled view.

4. Open the File menu and select Save Workbook.
   A Workbook Contents document opens, overlaid by the Save as dialogue
   box. The default name is BOOK1.XLW.
   Save the workbook as HOTELS.

5. Now exit from Excel.

6. Start Excel again and select the workbook name HOTELS.XLW.
   The worksheets contained in the workbook are all opened automatically and
   the contents page displayed.

7. Select the worksheet SUMMARY1 from the contents page.
   At the bottom right-hand corner of the sheet are three special buttons;

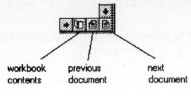

Figure 4.14

Click the first one – the contents page is re-displayed. Two buttons at the bottom left of the screen allow you to add or remove documents from the workbook.

These documents may be charts, worksheets or macro sheets. (removing a document from the workbook, or deleting the workbook itself, leaves the constituent documents unchanged)

The Options button allows you to define documents as,

bound – may only appear in one workbook, or
unbound – may appear in several workbooks

8. Click the Minimise button on the contents page.
    The workbook documents are displayed.

9. Select the document BUDGMAS.
    Click the Next Document button; the next 'page' of the workbook is displayed.
    Any individual document can be reduced, enlarged or restored by using the usual Minimise, Maximise, or Restore buttons at the top right of the document window.

10. Select the Previous Document icon; the previous document is re-displayed.

11. Now open the File menu and choose Close Workbook.
    All the documents in the work book are closed in one operation.

Summary of Commands and Functions

Notes: Menu commands show the menu name first, followed by the command to choose from the menu, e.g. Edit-Clear means open the Edit menu and select the Clear command.

Commands

Data-Table	Create a table from selected cells
File-Print Report	Print Excel report
File-New-Workbook	Create Workbook
New-Worksheet	Open new worksheet
File-Save Workbook	Save a workbook
Format-Border	Add border to selected cells
Format-Cell Protection	Protect selected cells
Formula-Define Name	Name a cell/range of cells
Formula-Goal Seek	Change values of selected cell so formula achieves a specified target value
Formula-Paste Function	Insert a selected function into a cell
Formula-Scenario Manager	Save selected ranges of variables from What If or Solver
Formula-Select Special	Select cells with specified contents
Formula-Solver	Use Solver
Formula-What If	Use What If macro
Options-Protect Document	Protect document
Options-Unprotect Document	Remove protection from document
Excel 3 Only.	
Window-Arrange All	Arrange documents on screen
Window-Show Information	Show information on a selected cell
Excel 4 Only.	
Options-Workspace-Info. Window	Show information on a selected cell
Window Arrange	Arrange documents on screen

Some Additional Functions.

Functions require you to supply information for their operations. These are called arguments.

e.g SUM(range) requires the argument, cell range, to be added. Arguments must be enclosed in brackets.

Optional arguments are shown in the lists that follow in square brackets – [ ] These brackets are for your guidance only and should not be typed. Function arguments are separated by commas. The commas must be typed.

Information Functions

COLUMNS(range)	counts the number of columns in a specified range
ISBLANK(value) ISNUMBER(value) ISTEXT(value)	IS functions check the type of value in a cell and report TRUE or FALSE accordingly, depending on whether the cell is blank, text etc.

Text Functions

EXACT(string1,string2)	Compares two text strings. Reports TRUE if they are the same or FALSE if they differ.
LEN(string)	Counts the number of characters in a text string.

Chapter 5: Automating Excel

Introduction to the Chapter

This chapter introduces the last main element of Excel-macros. A macro lets you save and re-use the commands that you issue by storing them up in a special macro sheet. The commands can then be run automatically whenever one needs them.

There are several advantages to using macros:

Saving Time. Issuing the same series of commands repeatedly is time consuming

Reducing Error. Long sequences of commands, mouse movements, and menu choices can be error prone. A macro achieves a consistent, correct result.

Controlling User Input. In a commercial situation users of varying skill and knowledge may be using the same worksheet model. The designer of the model wants to prevent users destroying data, amending formulae, or modifying assumptions.

Macros allow the designer to place limits on what users of worksheets can do; e.g. to disable certain menu choices, add custom menus and dialogue boxes, and at its most complex, design a complete custom-built system.

In this chapter we shall be starting with some simple macros which automate simple tasks.

In Chapter 6 we shall be building a complete user application.

Summary of Skills Covered

Skill	Activity	Skill	Activity
Button – creating	5	Macros – recording	1.2
Button – deleting	5.8	Macros – running	1.8, 2.8
Button – modifying	5.6	Macros – set recorder	2.3
Macros – automatic running	6	Macros – stop recording	1.5
Macros – naming	1.2		

Activity 1. Creating a Simple Macro

You can create a simple macro by using the macro recorder. Actions such as menu choices, mouse movements and keystrokes are then recorded and can be 'played back' when required.

Our first macro will automate the simple repetitive task of saving a worksheet, something you should do every 10 minutes or so.

Rather than making the choice from a menu you can use a shortcut, say, pressing the Ctrl key and the letter S.

Hints and Rules for macros.

A macro is stored on a special macro sheet.

Macro sheets resemble ordinary worksheets, but are assigned the special extension .XLM

Many macros can be stored on one macro sheet.

Macros store commands as special macro functions. Macros can control worksheets, charts and databases. Every macro is saved and run under a different name.

The macro name can be up to 255 characters long, must begin with a letter, and can consist of letters, numbers, full stops and underscores.

Spaces are not allowed so underscores or full stops are often used instead.

Macro names are not case sensitive.

When a macro is created it is usually assigned a shortcut key – a single letter – as well as a name.

Pressing down the Ctrl key and keying this letter will run the macro.

The letter that you assign to a macro is case-sensitive, e.g. Holding down the Ctrl key and pressing small s would run a particular macro; pressing Ctrl and Capital S would not. This gives you a potential 52 shortcut key combinations.

1. **Recording a Macro**. Open the Worksheet SHARES.XLS.
   Open the Macro menu and choose Record.
   A Record Macro dialogue box appears.

2. Enter the name SAVE_WORKSHEET in the name box.
   Press the Tab key and enter s in the Key box.
   You have now assigned the key strokes Ctrl-s to run the macro SAVE_WORKSHEET.
   Excel 3 users go to section 4 now.

Excel 4 3. **Excel 4 Only**. Excel 4 users will notice that the dialogue box offers them the extra choice of a Global Macro Sheet.
   The global sheet is opened automatically whenever you start Excel, and can be used to store and run commonly-used macros.
   The other option, Macro Sheet opens a new macro sheet. If you use this option then you have to open the macro sheet whenever you want to run the macro.
   Click the Global Macro Sheet button.

4. Click the OK button. The Recording message appears at the bottom of the screen.
    All your actions are being recorded now, so don't issue any super-fluous commands.
    We are now ready to record the macro steps.
    Open the Save menu and select Save. (not Save as)

5. Open the Macro menu now and select Stop Recorder.
    The Recording message stops.
    You have now recorded your first macro, SAVE_WORKSHEET which auto-mates the Save command, using the shortcut keys Ctrl and s.
    Let's see how this has been recorded.

Excel 3 6. **Excel 3 Users**. Open the Window menu and select Macro1

Excel 4 6. **Excel 4 Users**. Open the Window menu and select Unhide then Global (whenever you first open Excel the Global worksheet is opened but remains hidden)

The macro sheet appears on the screen.
It has the special .XLM extension, but otherwise looks like an ordinary worksheet.
The macro SAVE_WORKSHEET uses three cells:
Cell A1 contains the macro name and shortcut key.
Cells A2 and A3 hold the actions recorded by the macro, stored as special macro functions =SAVE() and =RETURN() .
They save the worksheet and then return control to the user. Macro functions, like worksheet functions, begin with an = sign and end in ().
Every macro begins with the macro name and ends with the =RETURN() function.

7. **Documenting the Macro.** As the macro sheet may be used to store many macros it is a good idea to document each macro.
    Click cell B1 and enter the comment, 'saves current sheet' Your macro sheet should now look like Figure 5.1.

	A	B
1	save_worksheet (s)	saves current sheet
2	=SAVE()	
3	=RETURN()	
4		

Figure 5.1

8. **Running the Macro**. Return to the SHARES worksheet.
   Hold down the Ctrl key and press the s key.
   The hour-glass symbol will confirm that the macro has run and the worksheet is being saved. If the SHARES worksheet is stored on diskette then the disk light should come on as well.

Excel 3   **Excel 3 users only**. Save the macro sheet as SHORTCUT and close the macro sheet. Now try running the macro again (Ctrl-s).
   You will find that the macro will not work; you must open a macro sheet before you can run a macro stored on it.

Excel 4   **Excel 4 Users Only**. Return to the macro sheet and save and close it, using Close on the File menu.
   Now try running the macro again (Ctrl-s). It will not run.
   Once the special GLOBAL macro sheet has been closed during an Excel session it will need to be opened, like any other macro sheet, before any macros can be run from them.

9. Now open the macro sheet again.
   Open the worksheet BUDGMAS too and make it the active worksheet.
   Now run the macro again – you will find that the macro will work on any Excel worksheet. (more specific macros will not as we will see later)

10. **Saving Macro Sheets**. Macro sheets can be saved, edited, opened, closed and deleted in the same way as a worksheet.

11. Save and close all worksheets and macro sheets.

Activity 2. Adding Macros to your Macro Sheet

> We are going to create a macro that will add the current date and time to a worksheet.
> It will automate the processes of typing the NOW() function into a cell and then converting it to a suitable date format.

1. Open the worksheet DISCT1.XLS and either the macro sheet
   SHORTCUT.XLM (Excel 3) or GLOBAL.XLM (Excel 4).

Excel 4   **Excel 4 Users only**. The GLOBAL macro sheet is opened automatically when you start Excel but is hidden.
   To display it open the Window menu and select Unhide

2. Open the Windows menu and select Arrange or Arrange All to display the two sheets side by side.
    Re-size them if necessary.

3. When you have started a new Excel session and want to add a new macro to an existing macro sheet you must do two things:

    a. Firstly the macro sheet must be open – we have already done this.

    b. Secondly we must indicate the place on the macro sheet where the macro is to start. (if you don't do this it will start in the next available column in the macro sheet)
        Click cell A5 on the macro sheet.
        Open the Macro menu and select Set Recorder.

4. Now select cell A1 on the DISCT1 worksheet.
    Open the Macro menu and select Record.
    Call the macro DATE_TIME and type d in the Key box.
    Click OK.
    The macro name should appear in cell A5 of the macro sheet. If it doesn't then you need to repeat the above steps.

5. Next type the function =NOW() in cell A1 of the worksheet and press Enter.
    Choose Number from the Format menu.
    Select the format d/m/yy h:mm (if you don't have this format then you can type it in the Format Box as a special 'custom' format)
    Click OK.
    The date appears, correctly formatted, in cell A1 of the DISCT1 worksheet.
    The macro formula appears in the macro sheet. Open the Macro menu and select Stop Recorder.

6. Select the macro sheet now.
    Widen the columns so that all the text is visible.
    Add a comment line in bold – see Figure 5.2.

	A	B
1	save_worksheet (s)	saves current sheet
2	=SAVE()	
3	=RETURN()	
4		
5	date_time (d)	**inserts date & time**
6	=FORMULA("=NOW()")	
7	=FORMAT.NUMBER("d/m/yy h:mm")	
8	=RETURN()	
9		
10		

Figure 5.2

7. Provided the macro sheet is open, you can add the date and time to any worksheet using the shortcut keys Ctrl-d.
    Close and save the DISCT1 worksheet.
    Open the worksheet MORTGAGE and, using the macro, add the date to cell A1.
    You may need to widen the column for the date and time to display properly.

8. **Running a Macro from the Menu**. If you forget the shortcut keys to run a macro then you can call it by name. Open the Macro menu and choose Run. Then choose the macro and click OK.
    Run the macro Save_Worksheet in this way.
    Close the MORTGAGE worksheet.

9. **Troubleshooting – If Your Recording Fails.....**
    The Excel Macro Recorder will record all your commands and key strokes – right or wrong.
    If you make a mistake while recording a simple macro then it is best to stop recording, return to the macro sheet, clear all the cells holding the macro, and start again.

10. **Recap – The Steps in Creating a Macro**.
    ❐ Open the macro sheet – or start a new one
    ❐ Select the cell where the macro is to start and select Set Recorder (optional)
    ❐ Activate the worksheet that the macro will control
    ❐ Open the Macro menu and select Record
    ❐ Name the macro and allocate the shortcut letter
    ❐ Record the actions in the macro
    ❐ Open the Macro menu and select Stop Recorder
    ❐ Run the macro to test it
    ❐ Add comments to the macro sheet

Activity 3. Opening a New Macro Sheet

> So far we have created our macros on one sheet, either GLOBAL if you are an Excel 4 user, or SHORTCUT if you are using Excel 3.
> This causes no problems for a group of small or related macros, but if a macro sheet becomes overlarge then it can occupy a lot of main memory and become difficult to scroll through.
> We will create a new macro sheet PRINT_IT that can store print macros. These will automate the printing of a worksheet.

1. Open the File menu and select New.
   Take the Macro Sheet option.
   Now open the worksheet MORTGAGE.

2. Open the Macro menu and choose Record.
   Call the macro PRINT_MORTGAGE and assign the short key m. Click OK.

3. The recording message appears at the bottom of the worksheet; record the following operations:
   Select the cells to be printed.
   Use the Options menu to set the print area.
   Open the File menu and select Page Setup. Set the left and right margins to 1 inch.
   Make sure that your printer is turned on and connected.
   Select Print; choose 1 copy and whatever other settings you wish.

4. Printing will now take place; when it is finished open the macro menu and choose Stop Recorder.
   You have now created a print macro on a new macro sheet.

5. Open the Window menu and select the new macro sheet
   It will have the default name Macro1 or similar – see Figure 5.3
   Add a suitable comment to document the macro –

	A
1	print_mortgage (m)
2	=FORMULA("")
3	=SELECT("R1C1:R17C3")
4	=SET.PRINT.AREA()
5	=PAGE.SETUP("&f","Page &p",1,1,1,1,FALSE,TRUE,FALSE,FALSE)
6	=PRINT(1,,,1,FALSE,FALSE,1,FALSE,1)
7	=RETURN()

Figure 5.3

Save the macro sheet as PRINT_IT; it can be used to store other print macros.

6. Return to the MORTGAGE worksheet.
    Test out your macro using the shortcut keys Ctrl-m.

Activity 4. Consolidation

An unavoidable limitation of the PRINT_MORTGAGE macro that we have just created is that it only applies to one specific worksheet – MORTGAGE.XLS.
This is because it sets a print area that is unlikely to apply to any other worksheet.
So each worksheet needs its own print macro

1. Open the worksheet HELPERS and make sure that the macro sheet PRINT_IT is still open.
    Now, using the operations in Activities 2 and 3 as a guide, add a new macro to print off the HELPERS worksheet.
    Call the macro PRINT_HELPERS and assign the shortcut key h to it.

Activity 5. Assigning a Macro to a Button

So far we have run macros either by pressing shortcut keys, (Ctrl plus a letter) or by using the Run command from the Macro menu.
An easier way of running the macro is to create a button on screen for the user to Click.
This will execute the macro directly, without needing to remember key presses or menu choices.

1. We will create a button to run the macro PRINT_MORTGAGE.
    Open the macro sheet PRINT_IT and the worksheet MORTGAGE.
    MORTGAGE should be the active sheet.

2. Look at the tool bar at the top of the screen.
    There is a button tool shaped like a small rounded rectangle on the far right of the Excel 3 tool bar – see the diagram at the end of Chapter 1.

3. **Creating the Button**. Click the button tool on the tool bar. The screen pointer changes to cross hairs.
    Scroll rows 19 and 20 of the worksheet into view if necessary.
    Position the screen pointer over the top left hand corner of cell B19.
    Drag the screen pointer so that the box covers cells B19 and B20.

Let go the mouse button and the button is drawn with the default name 'Button'.

We can reposition it later if necessary.

4. **Assigning a Macro to the Button**. The Assign to Object dialogue box opens automatically; select the macro name PRINT_MORTGAGE then the OK button.

   The macro is now assigned; if you could not find the macro name then cancel the dialogue box and check that you have opened the macro sheet.

5. **Labelling the Button.** To change the size and colour of the button, or the text that appears on it, first you must select it.

   Hold down the Ctrl key and click the button.

   Selection handles appear round the button.

   First change the text; erase the default name then open the Format menu and select Font.

   Choose 8 point.

   Click the Colour option and select a colour for the button.

   Click OK.

   The button should be still selected; type the label on the button 'Click to Print'.

   Click elsewhere on the worksheet to deselect the button.

6. **Moving or Sizing the Button**. Hold down the Ctrl key and click the button – selection handles appear.

   To alter the size drag one of the selection handles – the screen pointer will become + shaped.

   To move the button place the screen pointer on the edge of the button – not on a selection handle – and drag.

   The button can now be moved. (don't move the button within the print area or the button outline will be printed along with the worksheet)

7. **Re-assigning a Button**. If necessary you can assign a button to a new macro at any time.

   Select the button as before, then open the Macro menu and select the option Assign to Object.

8. **Deleting a Button**. If you have made a mess of your button, or no longer need it, then you can delete it. Select the button as before, then open the Edit menu and select Clear.

9. **Running the Macro**. If you are happy with the appearance of your button and that it is correctly assigned then try running it.

   Move the screen pointer on top of the button – the screen pointer becomes hand-shaped.

   Click once and the worksheet should print as before.

10. Save and close the macro sheet and the worksheet.

11. **Consolidation**. In Activity 4 you created the macro PRINT_HELPERS to print the worksheet HELPERS.
    Create and assign a print button for this worksheet too.

Activity 6. Running a Macro Automatically

> In the previous activity we created a button that had a macro assigned to it.
> Clicking the button called the macro which in turn printed part of the worksheet.
> It would be even better if the macro sheet opened automatically when the worksheet that uses it opens. (as we have seen, if you forget to open the macro sheet then the macro will not run)
> To do this we define a name on the worksheet beginning with Auto_Open.

1. Open the worksheet MORTGAGE.XLS.

2. Open the Formula menu and select Define Name.

3. A dialogue box appears; select the Name box and type the name Auto_Open.

4. Select the Refers to box next.
   It must contain the name of the macro sheet that you are calling, plus the name of the macro.
   Type =PRINT_IT.XLM!PRINT_MORTGAGE and click OK. (the ! symbol connects the two part of the formula)

5. Save and close MORTGAGE.XLS and the macro sheet PRINT_IT.

6. Now open MORTGAGE.XLS again.
   The macro sheet should open as well and the table begin to print. Cancel this if you wish.

7. **Trouble Shooting**. If you get an error message then check the following:

   ❑ Open the Formula menu and select Define Name again
     Check the spelling and syntax of the entries in the dialogue box for the name Auto_Open – there must be no spaces, you must use the underscore (_) not the dash, and the ! symbol must be included to denote an external reference.

   ❑ Are the worksheet and the macro sheet on the same drive?

If not then the drive must appear in the Refers to box, e.g.
=A:\PRINT_IT.XLM!PRINT_MORTGAGE

Now save and close the worksheet and try again!

8. It is a definite advantage to have the macro sheet open automatically when the worksheet is opened.
   However we probably will not want the macro to start printing the worksheet automatically as it does at the moment; we only want the worksheet to print when we click the button.
   It is quite easy to fix this.
   Open the macro sheet PRINT_IT and look at the final cell of the PRINT_MORTGAGE macro; it contains the function =RETURN() which returns control to the user when the macro ends.
   Make a note of the cell reference, it should be A7 or similar.

9. Now activate the MORTGAGE worksheet again.
   Open the Formula menu and select Define Name.
   Select the name Auto_Open again
   Amend the Refers to reference to =PRINT_IT.XLM!$A$7 (or whatever the cell reference is – the $ signs represent an absolute reference)

10. Exit and save the macro and work sheets.

11. Now open the worksheet MORTGAGE again – this time the macro sheet still opens but the macro itself will not run.
    This is because we have amended the external reference to go straight to the final line of the macro and skip the cells which control the printing – A1 to A6.
    Use the Window menu to test that the macro sheet has in fact opened and test the button again.

12. **Additional Notes**

    ❑ It is also possible to run a macro automatically when a you close a worksheet; use steps 1 to 5 above, but in the Name box type a name that begins with Auto_Close.

    ❑ More than one macro can be run automatically from the same worksheet. Each name must begin with Auto_Close or Auto_Open, e.g. Auto_Open_Print or Auto_Close_Print.

13. **Consolidation**. Open the worksheet HELPERS.XLS.
    Using the above operations, make the macro sheet PRINT_IT open automatically when the worksheet is opened.

Summary of Commands

Notes: Menu commands show the menu name first, followed by the command to choose from the menu, e.g. Edit-Clear means open the Edit menu and select the Clear command.

Commands

Ctrl-[letter]	run macro using shortcut key
Ctrl-[select]	select screen button
Macro-Assign to Object	assign macro to button
Macro-Run	run a macro
Macro-Record	create and record a macro
Macro-Set Recorder	select a cell on macro sheet for macro to start recording
Macro-Stop Recorder	stop recording a macro
Window-Unhide	display a hidden document

Chapter 6: Designing a User Application

Introduction to the Chapter

In the previous chapter you created a number of simple macros that automated small tasks such as printing and saving a worksheet.

In this chapter we are going to use macros to automate a whole application – maintaining records of purchase orders. Every time a company orders goods it sends out a purchase order to a supplier. It needs to keep a record of these and to set up a database for the purpose. This means purchase order records will need to be added to the database, as well as edited, saved and printed.

This application may well be used by people unfamiliar with Excel, who cannot be expected to use the normal menus, commands etc.

Macros are the binding material that will hold the parts of the system together and present it to the user in a simple way.

Overview of the Application

It is important to plan the application, at least in general outline, before starting on the worksheet and macros.

Use this section to guide you through the various parts of the system before you start on the first activity.

1. The first screen that the user will see is a specially designed title screen – see Figure 6.2
    This offers a special custom menu at the top of the screen and a title display. Several macros are used for this screen, e.g. to set off normal screen defaults such as gridlines and tool bars and to display the custom menu.

2. A custom dialogue box is also designed for the user to enter purchase order details, e.g Supplier Name, Quantity, Product, Price – see Figure 6.7
    The specifications for this dialogue box are held in the macro sheet – see Figure 6.9.

3. The data entered in this dialogue box are transferred to a database, using a macro – see Figure 6.14.

4. Users will be able to edit the data records where necessary using a standard data form. This too can be called by a macro.

5.   Such an application can look daunting; don't worry, it can be built up and tested piece by piece.
     At the end you will have a worthwhile application that can be added to as needs demand.

Summary of Skills Covered

Skill	Activity	Skill	Activity
Cells – naming	7.3, 16.3	Dialogue Boxes – Displaying	5.7
Conditions – testing	16	Dialogue Boxes – Editing	6
Custom Menus – creating	12	Macros – Testing	3, 16.2
Custom Screens – creating	1	Response Box – Creating	16
Data Forms – displaying	10	Screens – Positioning	2
Dialogue Boxes – Clearing	15	Screen Defaults – Setting	2
Dialogue Boxes – Creating	4, 15	User Choice – Testing	16

Activity 1. Creating User Screens

> We will create the title screen first – see Figure 6.2. We will not add the custom menu until a later activity.

1.   Open a new worksheet and, using Figure 6.1 as a guide, amend the sizes of the columns and rows as follows:
     Column A to 17.00 wide
     Columns B and H to 0.50 wide
     Row 1 to 50.00 high
     Rows 3,9 and 19 to 3.00 high.

     Hint. You can use alter their sizes directly using the screen pointer, or use the Format menu; you can undo mistakes using the Undo option on the Edit menu.

     The narrow rows and columns now form a box on screen.

2.   Select cell range B3 to B19 – the left side of the box.
     Open the Format menu and select Border.
     A dialogue box appears; select the Outline option.
     You can also select colour if you wish.
     Click OK.
     Select cell range H3 to H19 – the right side of the box.
     Open the Edit option and select Repeat Border.

3. Next we can complete the horizontal sides of the box.
   Repeat the above operations for the cell ranges B3 to H3 and B19 to H19.
   Compare your results with Figure 6.1

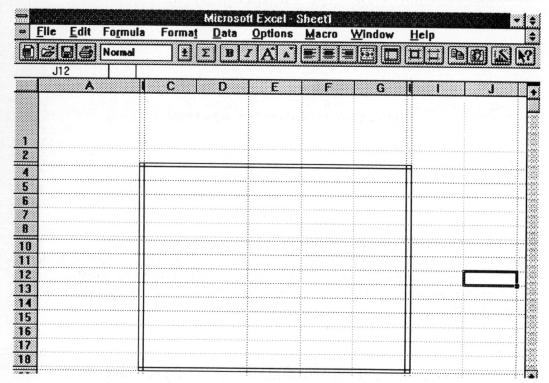

Figure 6.1

4. Now save the worksheet as ORDENTER.XLS.

5. We can now enter text in the box.
   Select cell C6.
   Open the Format menu and select Font.
   Choose 14 point Bold.
   Now with cell C6 still selected, type the title, PURCHASE ORDER
   SYSTEM and press Enter.
   Centre this title across cells C6 to G6 (see Chapter 1, Activity 2)
   Now select cell range C4 to G8.
   Open the Format menu and select Border.
   Select the Shade option.

6. Select cell C14 and type the user message,
   'Use the Orders Menu to Add, Edit or Print'
   Outline the range of cells containing this message, and embolden and centre
   it as before.
   Your screen should resemble Figure 6.2.

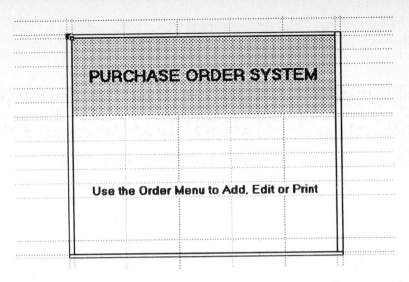

Figure 6.2

7. Now that we have defined our title screen we can create the screen for the purchase order database. This will hold records of items supplied.
Scroll down to cell L26 and enter the column headings shown in Figure 6.3.
Embolden and centre the headings.
Press Ctrl-Home to go to the top of the worksheet.

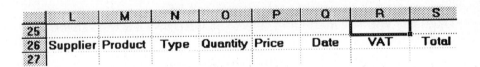

	L	M	N	O	P	Q	R	S
25								
26	Supplier	Product	Type	Quantity	Price	Date	VAT	Total
27								

Figure 6.3

Activity 2. Macros Which Format Screens

We now have the title and the database screens and can record macros to control them. We will use the same recording techniques that we used in the previous chapter, so I shall be keeping instructions and explanations to a minimum.

Remember the basic steps in creating a macro:

- ☐ Open the macro sheet
- ☐ Select the cell where the macro is to start and select Set Recorder
- ☐ Activate the worksheet that the macro will control
- ☐ Open the Macro menu and select Record
- ☐ Name the macro and allocate the shortcut letter
- ☐ Record the actions in the macro
- ☐ Open the Macro menu and select Stop Recorder
- ☐ Add comments and test

1. Open the File menu and select New.
   Select the Macro Sheet option and click OK.

2. A new macro sheet is displayed; narrow column A to 5.00 and widen column B to 27.
   Only columns A-C should be visible now.
   Select cell B6 on the macro sheet.
   Open the Macro menu and select Set Recorder.
   The macro will now start recording at cell B6.
   Open the Window menu and select the ORDENTER worksheet.

3. Our first macro will format the title screen that we have just created.
   Open the Macro menu and select Record; type the macro name Format_Sheet.
   Assign the letter a as the shortcut key. Click OK.
   From now on your actions are being recorded!

4. Open the Options menu and select Display.
   Click the two boxes Gridlines and Row and Column Headings to deselect them. Click OK.
   Open the Options menu again and select the Workspace option; deselect the following 4 options:
   Scroll Bar, Status Bar, Formula Bar and Toolbars.

Excel 4 **Excel 4 only.** Turn off the Tool Bar by choosing Tool Bar from the Options menu. Then select the Hide option.

5. Click the top left corner of the box that surrounds the title SALES ORDER
   ENTRY, i.e. cell B3.
   This 'parks' the screen pointer in an inconspicuous place.

6. Open the Macro menu and choose Stop Recorder.
   The first macro is recorded.
   Use the Window menu to return to the macro sheet.
   Add the comments shown in Figure 6.4

	B	C
1		
2		
3		
4		
5		
6	Format_Sheet (a)	format entry screen
7	=DISPLAY(FALSE,FALSE,FALSE,TRUE,0,TRUE,FALSE,1)	
8	=WORKSPACE(FALSE,FALSE,FALSE,FALSE,FALSE,"/",FALSE	turn off gridline etc
9	=SHOW.TOOLBAR(1,FALSE)	turn off toolbar
10	=SELECT("R3C2")	park cursor
11	=RETURN()	

Figure 6.4

Save the macro sheet as ORDCTRL.XLM

7. The second macro will reverse the effects of the first.
   i.e. it will restore the normal screen defaults before the database screen is
   displayed.
   Select cell B13 on the macro sheet.
   Open the Macro menu and select Set Recorder.
   Open the Window menu and select the ORDENTER worksheet.

8. Open the Macro menu and select Record.
   Name the macro Restore_Screen.
   Enter the letter b in the Key box. Click OK.
   Your actions are now being recorded.

9. Now repeat the operations described in section 4 above
   By selecting the options again you will restore the default settings.

10. Open the Macro menu and choose Stop Recorder.
    The second macro is recorded.
    Use the Window menu to return to the macro sheet.
    Add the comments shown in Figure 6.5

	B	C
12		
13	Restore_Screen (b)	restore defaults
14	=DISPLAY(FALSE,TRUE,TRUE,TRUE,0,,TRUE,FALSE,1)	
15	=WORKSPACE(FALSE,,FALSE,,TRUE,TRUE,TRUE,"",FALSE,F	turn on gridlines etc
16	=SHOW.TOOLBAR(1,TRUE)	turn on toolbar
17	=RETURN()	
18		

Figure 6.5

11. We now need two more macros to set up and position the title and the database screens.
Select cell B20 on the macro sheet and Set Recorder as before.

12. Use the Window menu to display the worksheet; choose Record from the Macro menu.
Call the macro Set_Title_Page and assign the letter c.
Click OK. You are now recording.
Press down the Ctrl and Home keys together – the cursor moves to cell A1, the 'home' position.
Click the top left corner of the box surrounding the title – cell B3 – to park the cursor.
Stop recording now and return to the macro sheet.
The third macro is recorded

13. Select cell B25 on the macro sheet and Set Recorder as before. This is where the fourth macro will start.
Use the Window menu to display the worksheet.
Choose Record from the Macro menu.
Call the macro Set_Database_Page and assign the letter d.
You are now recording.

14. Scroll down until row 26 appears at the top of the screen; this row contains the database titles.
Scroll across the worksheet until column k is the left-most column; all the headings should be displayed now. (see Figure 6.3)
Click the Maximise button if necessary.
Stop recording now and return to the macro sheet.

15. Add the comments shown in Figure 6.6 to the two latest macros.

	B	C
19		
20	Set_Title_Page (c)	
21	=SELECT("R3C2")	go to cell A1
22	=RETURN()	
23		
24		
25	Set_Database_page (d)	
26	=VLINE(25)	go to row 26
27	=HLINE(10)	align col K to left
28	=RETURN()	

Figure 6.6

Activity 3. Testing Macros

1. Return to the worksheet:
    Press Ctrl-c – the title screen is positioned
    Press Ctrl-a – the title screen is formatted
    Press Ctrl-b – the normal screen settings are restored
    Press Ctrl-d – the database screen is displayed
    Warning. Don't run a macro unless the worksheet is the active document. If you run a macro when the macro sheet is active you may end up re-formatting the macro sheet. As you cannot undo such an error you must either re-format the macro sheet manually, or exit from the macro sheet without saving it.

2. **Stepping Through a Macro.** It is possible to execute a macro one step at a time; this is useful for testing and debugging.
    With the worksheet selected, press Ctrl-c to go to the title screen.
    Open the Macro menu and select the Run option.
    Select the macro Set_Database_Page from the list displayed

    The Single Step dialogue box appears.
    Click the Step or Step Into button – the first line of the macro executes.
    Click Step or Step Into again; the step executes and the worksheet changes.
    Continue until the macro is completed.

    Other Step options.
    The Evaluate button evaluates the formula of the current line.
    The Halt button cancels the macro.
    The Continue button executes the rest of the macro as normal without stepping.

3. **Correcting a Macro.** If one of your macros is not working properly there are various options:

a. You can edit the line of the macro – this can be very difficult for a complex function unless you fully understand its syntax – better to either,

b. Delete the whole macro and start again – select the relevant macro lines on the macro sheet and use the Clear command, or,

c. Delete the lines of the macro from the incorrect line(s) to the end, then start recording again as follows:
Select the next line of the macro sheet and select Set Recorder from the Macro menu
Display the worksheet and start the recorder again. Record the actions again.
Stop the recorder, and add comments to the macro sheet

Remember to test your macros after you have amended them.

Activity 4. Creating a Dialogue Box

We have designed our first two screens and four macros to control them.
The next step is to design a special 'custom' dialogue box to allow the user to enter records into the orders database.
Figure 6.7 shows the completed dialogue box.

A special dialogue editor allows us to create dialogue boxes with all the Excel features of buttons, check boxes and scroll bars.
The dialogue box specifications can then be copied to the macro sheet and a macro can be written to call up the dialogue box.

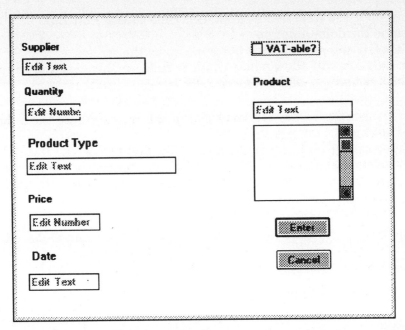

Figure 6.7

1. **Entering the Editor**. Make sure that the macro sheet ORDCTRL is open. In the top left-hand corner of the screen is a feature that we have so far ignored – the Control menu icon – it is a grey box with a rectangular handle. (there may be two – one for the sheet and one for the whole screen. If so choose the upper one)
Open this menu and select the Run option.
Select Dialogue Editor.
A blank dialogue box is displayed on screen, ready to be designed.
Three menus appear at the top of the Editor screen – File, Edit, and Item.

2. Move the screen pointer onto the bottom right-hand corner of the blank box and drag to enlarge it by about 50% – don't worry about exact sizes at this stage – all boxes can be moved and re-sized by the usual dragging method.

3. **Adding Labels and Edit Boxes**. We are now going to create the data entry boxes that will add the data items to the database – supplier, quantity etc.
Open the Item menu and select the Text option; a text box appears on the dialogue box.
Type the heading Supplier.
Hint. Now drag this text box away from the top of the dialogue box – see Figure 6.7 for guidance.
If it is too near it can become confused with the title of the dialogue box.

4. Now open the Item menu again, this time choose Edit Box.
Text is the default option.
Click OK and an Edit Text box appears on the screen.
An edit box will allow you to enter details, in this case the supplier's name which is text, i.c. alphanumeric data.

5. Now select Text from the Item menu again and create the second heading **Quantity**.
Now open the Item menu and select Edit Box.
This time click the Number option plus OK. (quantity is a numeric field)

6. Now create the heading **Product Type** and a text field.

7. Now create two more fields **Price**, a numeric field, and **Date**, a text field.

8. **Correcting Mistakes**. If you wish to delete a box or text, simply click it to select it then choose Clear from the Edit menu.
To edit a box open the Edit menu and select the Info option.

9. **Adding a Check Box**. We need to enter a check box so that the user can enter whether VAT is due on an item.
As most items are VAT-able an X will appear in the box by default, if the user deselects it then VAT is not payable.
Open the Item menu and select Button; a dialogue box appears.
Click the Check Box option and then OK.

10. Now we need to name and position the check box.
Open the Edit menu and select the Info option.
A dialogue box appears on the screen.
Make the entries shown in Figure 6.8 and click OK.

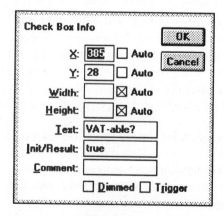

Figure 6.8

The values in the X and Y boxes show the horizontal and vertical position of the check box.

The logical value TRUE in the Int/Result box ensures that the check box is checked by default.

11. **Adding a List Box**. The list box will contain items of stock that can be added to the database.

    Open the Item menu and choose List Box. Click the Linked option then OK. A list box appears on screen.

    The main box will contain a list of products;the scroll bars will allow you to find and select the one you want.

    The text box above the list box is linked to it and will contain the item currently selected in the list box, or allow you to type a new one.

    Make sure that these two linked boxes do not become separated.

    Choose Text from the Item menu and type the heading **Product** over the text box.

12. **Adding Buttons.** All we need to add now are the Enter and Cancel buttons – see Figure 6.7.

    These buttons will you either to enter a record or to cancel the entry.

    Open the Item menu and select Button; click OK to accept the default.

    The button is labelled OK at the moment, change this to Enter and drag the button under the list box.

    Open the Item menu and select the Button option again.

    This time the default offered is Cancel; click OK to accept this and reposition the button.

13. Now reposition all the elements in the completed screen to achieve a neat layout, using Figure 6.7 as a guide.

    Figure 6.7 also gives an approximate guide to the lengths of the edit fields.

Activity 5. Adding the Dialogue Box to the Macro Sheet

1. All the dialogue box specifications must be copied to the macro sheet.

   Open the Edit menu and choose the Select Dialogue option, Then open the Edit menu and select Copy.

   Use the Minimise button – top right of document – to shrink the Dialogue Editor.

   The macro sheet ORDCTRL should be revealed, if not use the Window menu.

   Activate the cell D5 on the macro sheet.

2. Open the Edit menu and select Paste.

   All the specifications for the dialogue box are copied to the macro sheet.

   Scroll across the macro sheet and you will find that they occupy 7 columns – D to J; to have typed them in yourself would have been a formidable task!

3. Narrow the columns so that they can all be seen on screen.
   Briefly explained, the columns contain the following specifications:
   Column D contains code numbers for each type of dialogue item;
   1 = OK button,
   5 = text,
   6 = text box,
   8 = number box,
   13 = check box
   16 = linked list box.
   Columns E and F give the position of each item as X and Y coordinates.
   Columns G and H give the height and width of each item.
   Hint. These two sets of coordinates may be amended on the macro sheet, so that, e.g. text and boxes are at a standard X coordinate, or a standard height.
   Column I contains the text headings for each item.
   Column J contains the initial settings or results of a dialogue box, i.e. any data that has been entered in the boxes.
   Now, using Figure 6.9 as a guide, type headings in row 4 for these 7 columns.

	D	E	F	G	H	I	J
4	Item Type	X Coord	Y Coord	Width	Height	Text	Values
5				608	332		
6				734	332		
7	5	14	53			Supplier	
8	6	14	74	198			
9	5	14	112			Quantity	
10	5	14	167			Product Type	
11	6	14	192	241			
12	5	14	272			Date	
13	6	14	296	113			
14	5	14	218			Price	
15	8	14	244	113			
16	13	386	68			VAT-able?	TRUE
17	6	386	117	160			
18	16	386	149	160	84		
19	5	386	93			Products	
20	1	386	243			Enter	
21	2	386	286	88		Cancel	
22	8	20	140	89			

Figure 6.9

The cell references in your macro sheet may be slightly different to the ones shown in the figure. If so you will have to adjust some of the cell references mentioned in these activities accordingly.

4. **Entering the List of Products**. Scroll across to cell K17 and enter the list of products shown in Figure 6.10

	J	K
16		
17		WordPerfect 5.1
18		Excel 4
19		Lotus 123
20		PC Tools
21		Windows 3.1
22		Dbase IV
23		dBase III
24		MSDOS 5
25		dBASE Manual
26		Excel Workbook
27		dBASE User Guide
28		Lotus 123 Manual

Figure 6.10

5. We now need to name the range of cells containing these products and link it to the list box on the dialogue box. This ensures that the products appear in the list box.
   Open the Formula menu and select Define Name; a dialogue box appears.
   Enter the name as Products and then move to the Refers to box.
   Give the cell range holding the list of products the absolute references $K$17:$K$28 and then click OK.

6. The next step requires some care.
   Look in column D of the macro sheet for item type 16. This is the linked list item on the dialogue box.
   Now read along the row and find the blank cell in column I.
   In Figure 6.9 it is cell I17, yours may be slightly different.
   This is the cell that needs linking to the product list. Select the cell and enter ORDCTRL.XLM!PRODUCTS (n.b. there is no = sign, this is not a formula)
   This ties the product list – named Product – to the text box of the list box.

7. **Creating a Macro to Call a Dialogue Box**.
   We now need to write a short macro that will call up the dialogue box.
   Select cell D1 and type the macro name, Call_Dialogue_Box. Press Enter.
   Open the Formula menu and select the Define Name option. A dialogue box appears, click the Command button.
   Enter e in the Ctrl + box to define the shortcut key. Click OK.
   In cell D2 enter the formula =DIALOG.BOX(but do not complete the bracket.
   Now, starting from cell D6, select the whole range of the cells that were copied over from the dialogue editor in sections 1 and 2. (don't include the column headings or the product list).
   This range is inserted into the formula in cell D2.
   Complete the formula by typing the final bracket.
   Press Enter.

The formula should read =DIALOG.BOX(D6:J22), but your cell range may be slightly different to this.

In cell D3 insert the final function =RETURN() to end the macro.

Your macro should now look like Figure 6.11

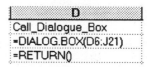

Figure 6.11

8. Now test the macro – press Ctrl-e.
   The macro should call up the dialogue box.
   Test that you can scroll through the list of products that appear in the list box and that you can move from field to field. Use the mouse or Tab key, but do not enter any data yet.
   Finally use the Cancel button to exit the dialogue box.

Activity 6. Editing the Dialogue Box

If the dialogue box is working to your satisfaction then skip this activity.
You may not be happy with the dialogue box now that you have seen it running.
If so, you will need to copy the definitions from the macro sheet back to the dialogue editor, amend them, then copy the amended dialogue box back to the macro sheet.

1. First select the range of cells in the macro sheet containing the dialogue box specifications.
   Open the Edit menu and select Copy.

2. Use the Control menu to run the Dialogue Editor – see Activity 4, section 1.
   On the dialogue editor screen select Paste from the Edit menu.
   The dialogue screen will be copied from the macro sheet.
   If you have copied the wrong range of cells then select Undo from the Edit menu and repeat the above steps.

3. Make your changes.
   Open the Edit menu and choose Select Dialogue.
   Open the Edit menu and choose Copy.
   Minimise the dialogue editor screen and return to the macro sheet.

4. The revised dialogue box definition may occupy a different number of cells than the original one.

As a precaution paste it to an empty area of the worksheet first and check its dimensions against the original, otherwise you may overwrite other macro cells.

5. If it is the same size then use the Clear command to delete the original definition. Then paste the new definition into its place.

6. If the number of cells has changed then you may also need to amend formula references to reflect this – see the previous activity.

Activity 7. Naming Data Cells in the Macro Sheet

1. Now use the dialogue box to enter the first record, using the following values. Use the mouse or Tab key to move from field to field.
    Click the Enter button on the dialogue box and you will return to the macro sheet.

Box	Value to Enter
Supplier	J M Software
Quantity	12
Product Type	Book
Price	15.50
Date	26-Aug
Products	(Scroll through the list box and select Excel Work book)

2. Scroll to column J in the macro sheet, headed Values and you will see that the data has been transferred to the macro sheet.
    This is what should happen, given that the dialogue box specifications now form part of the macro sheet.

3. We now need to name each data item so that it can be transferred to the database.
    Select the cell in column J containing the text 'JM SOFTWARE'.
    Open the Formula menu and select Define Name,
    Name this cell SUPPLIER and click OK.

4. Repeat this naming operation as follows:
    Select the cell in column J containing the quantity 12.
    Name this cell QUANTITY.
    Select the cell in column J containing the product type Book.
    Name this cell TYPE.
    Select the cell in column J containing the price of 15.50.
    Name this cell PRICE.
    Select the cell in column J containing the date 26-Aug.
    Name this cell DATE.
    Select the cell in column J containing the logical value of TRUE.

Name this cell VATABLE.
Select the cell in column J containing the text 'Excel Workbook'.
Name this cell PRODUCT.

Activity 8. Transferring Data to the Database

> The dialogue box that we created in the previous activity allows a user to enter a data record.
> At the moment the data entered is stored in the macro sheet along with the macros and formulae.
> This is not particularly convenient or readable.
> Therefore we need to transfer the data into columns in the database that we have already set up – see Activity 1, Figure 1.3

1. Scroll the macro sheet and activate cell B33 (or the next available cell in column B)
   Open the macro menu and choose Set Recorder.

2. Open the worksheet ORDENTER now.
   Open the Macro menu and select the Record option.
   Call this macro Disp_Database and allocate the letter f as the shortcut key.
   Click OK and you are now recording.

3. Press Ctrl-a to call the title screen.
   Press Ctrl-d to display the database field headings.
   Now press Ctrl-b to reset the screen defaults.
   Scroll the screen up to row 22 so as to leave a few rows above the database headings.
   Click on the field heading 'Supplier' in cell L26.
   Stop the recorder now.

4. Return to the macro sheet.
   With added comments the Disp_Database macro looks like Figure 6.12

	B	C
32		
33	Disp_Database (f)	
34	=RUN("TESTCTRL.XLM!Format_Sheet",FALSE)	format title screen
35	=RUN("TESTCTRL.XLM!Set_Database_page",FALSE)	go to d'base screen
36	=RUN("TESTCTRL.XLM!Restore_Screen",FALSE)	restore settings
37	=VLINE(-4)	select 1st field heading
38	=SELECT("R26C12")	
39	=RETURN()	
40		

Figure 6.12

Note. Macros can not only record commands but can call other macros.

5. Now return to the worksheet ORDENTER and scroll up to row 22.
    We are going to use cells in this row to temporarily store database records transferred from the macro sheet.
    Then we will copy them down to the database area in row 27 onwards.

6. In cell L22 type the formula =ORDCTRL.XLM!SUPPLIER
    This formula refers to the cell in the macro sheet ORDCTRL named SUP-PLIER containing the value JM SOFTWARE.
    This value now appears in cell L22.
    If it does not, then check that the syntax and spelling of this formula.
    Also check that it matches the name given to the cell in the macro sheet – see Activity 7.

7. We need to create other similar linking formulae;
    In cell M22 type the formula =ORDCTRL.XLM!PRODUCT
    In cell N22 type the formula =ORDCTRL.XLM!TYPE
    In cell O22 type the formula =ORDCTRL.XLM!QUANTITY
    In cell P22 type the formula =ORDCTRL.XLM!PRICE
    In cell Q22 type the formula =ORDCTRL.XLM!DATE
    The actual values that are held in these cells in the macro sheet will appear as the formulae are executed.

8. We now need to enter formulae to calculate the VAT and the total price for the order record.
    The formula for VAT is the product of quantity, price and VAT rate (currently 17.5%)
    Enter the formula =O22*P22*0.175 in cell R22.

9. The total price is quantity multiplied by price, plus VAT,
    i.e. =(O22*P22)+R22 Enter this in cell S22.

10. Now we need to format the columns; select the column designators and format as follows:

Price, VAT, and Total columns to 2 decimal places
The Date column to d-mmm-yy.
The Quantity column to no decimal places(0).
Widen the columns where necessary.

Activity 9. Adding Records to the Database

We now need to define certain cells as the database area. (see Chapter 3)
We can then record a macro that adds records to it.

1. Select the 8 field names. (cells L26 to S26), **plus** the 2 rows of 8 cells directly underneath.
   You have now selected the cell range L26 to S28.
   Open the Data menu and select Set Database.

2. Now open the macro sheet ORDCTRL and scroll down to cell B42 (or the first available cell in this column)
   Open the Macro menu and choose Set Recorder.
   Return to the worksheet.
   Open the Macro menu and select the Record option.
   Call the macro Add_Order and assign the letter g as shortcut key.
   Click OK. You are now recording.

3. a. Click the row designator for row 27 – the whole row is selected.

   b. Open the Edit menu and select Insert – a blank page is inserted.

   c. Select the record in row 22 (cells L22 – S22)

   d. Open the Edit menu and select Copy – the record is framed by a 'marquee'.

   e. Click cell L27.

   f. Open the Edit menu and select Paste Special.

   g. Select the Values option, then click OK (the values, not the formulae are copied)

   h. Press the Esc key to remove the marquee.

   i. Open the macro menu and Stop Recorder.

Whenever this macro is run a blank row will be inserted in to the database area and the new record copied in from row 22 – see Figure 6.13

	L	M	N	O	P	Q	R	S
22	JM SOFTWARE	Excel Workbook	BOOK	12	15.50	26-AUG	32.55	218.55
23								
24								
25								
26	Supplier	Product	Type	Quantity	Price	Date	VAT	Total
27	JM SOFTWARE	Excel Workbook	BOOK	12	15.50	26-AUG	32.55	218.55
28								

Figure 6.13

4. Return to the macro sheet now.
   Your macro should resemble Figure 6.14
   Add the comments shown in the adjacent column.

	B	C
40		
41		
42	Add_Order (g)	adds rec to d'base
43	=SELECT("R27","R27C12")	select row 27
44	=INSERT(2)	insert new row
45	=SELECT("R22C12:R22C19")	select record in row 22
46	=COPY()	copy record
47	=SELECT("R27C12")	select new row 27
48	=PASTE.SPECIAL(3,1,FALSE,FALSE)	paste record
49	=RETURN()	

Figure 6.14

5. Now activate the worksheet again.
   Test the macro; press Ctrl-e to call the dialogue box. At the moment the data from the first record is still displayed – we will fix this later.
   Type in a new record over the existing record, using data of your own,
   Click the Enter button to complete entering the record. You are returned to the worksheet.
   Now press Ctrl-g, the new record is copied from the macro sheet into the database.
   Repeat the above operations until you have about 5 records in the database.
   You may need to adjust the column width of some of the database columns to accommodate some of the field lengths

6. **Consolidation**. We now need a macro to combine these two activities of using the dialogue box and adding the record to the database; i.e. joining up the macros Call_Dialogue-Box and Add-Order.
   Create this macro yourself:
   Call it Update-Database and allocate it the shortcut key x. It is simply a matter of recording the running of these two macros.

Activity 10 Using a Data Form

> Excel provides a standard form for you to add, delete, or edit records – see Chapter 3, Activity 4.

1. Open the macro sheet ORDCTRL and scroll down to cell B52 (or the first available cell in this column)
   Open the Macro menu and choose Set Recorder.
   Return to the worksheet.
   Open the Macro menu and choose Record.
   Call the macro Call_Form and assign the letter h as shortcut key. Click OK.
   You are now recording.

2. Open the Data menu and select Form – a data form is displayed.
   Click the Close button on the form.

3. Now press Ctrl-d and Control-a.
   The title screen appears.
   Stop the Recorder.
   Press Ctrl-b to restore the screen defaults.

4. Return to the macro sheet now.
   Your macro should resemble Figure 6.15

	A	B
51		
52		Call_Form (h)
53		=DATA.FORM()
54		=RUN("TESTCTRL.XLM!Set_Title_Page",FALSE)
55		=RUN("TESTCTRL.XLM!Format_Sheet",FALSE)
56		=RETURN()

Figure 6.15

Activity 11. Printing and Saving

> We will write two short macros – one to print the database and one to save the worksheet and macro sheet. Turn the printer on for this activity.

1. Open the macro sheet ORDCTRL and scroll down to cell B59 (or the first available cell in this column)
   Open the Macro menu and choose Set Recorder.
   Return to the worksheet.

Open the Macro menu and choose Record.
Call the macro Print_it and assign the letter i as shortcut key. Click OK.
You are now recording.

2. Press Ctrl-f to call the database screen.
    Select cell L26 – the first heading in the database.
    Hold down the Shift and Ctrl keys and press the down arrow key.
    Open the Formula menu and choose the Select Special option. Click the button labelled Current Region. Click OK.
    The whole database area should be selected.

3. Open the Options menu and select Set Print Area.
    Open the File menu and select Print – a dialogue box appears.
    Make any other choices from the dialogue box that you wish. Wait until the database has printed.
    Stop the Recorder.
    If the print-out is not to your satisfaction then you may need to adjust the page set up.
    Erase and re-record the macro – see Activity 3, section 3.

4. Now add another record and test the print macro.
    Make sure that the full database is printed, including the new record.

5. Now build a save and quit macro.
    The macro will save both worksheet and macro sheet and then quit Excel.
    Call the macro Save_Quit, assign the letter j and start recording.
    First save the worksheet.
    Close the worksheet – you are returned to the macro sheet. Save the macro sheet.
    Stop the recorder.

6. To complete this macro we need to insert a =QUIT() function before the =RETURN() function in order to quit Excel.
    Do this.
    Your macro should resemble Figure 6.16
    Add the comments shown in the adjacent column.

	B	C
67		
68	Save_Quit (j)	
69	=SAVE()	save worksheet
70	=FILE.CLOSE()	close worksheet
71	=SAVE()	save macro sheet
72	=QUIT()	quit excel
73	=RETURN()	

Figure 6.16

7. Open the worksheet and test the macro; it should save the both worksheet then the macro sheet and then exit Excel.

8. Run Excel again and open the worksheet and the macro sheet.

Activity 12. Creating the Custom Menu

We have created macros to run all the major database operations – adding records, updating and searching, printing the database and exiting.
We now need to design a custom menu that offers these options; it will resemble a standard Excel bar menu in appearance and operation.
We cannot use the macro Record feature for this; instead you must create a special menu table on the macro sheet. This requires some care in syntax and spelling.

1. Open the macro sheet ORDCTRL and scroll across so that column M is on the left of the screen – see Figure 6.17

	M	N	O	P	Q	
11	*Menu Options*	*Macros Called*		*Status Bar Messages*	*Custom Help*	
12						
13	Orders					
14	Enter an Order	Ordctrl.xdm!Update_Database		Enter a new order		
15	Edit an Order	Ordctrl.xdm!Call_Form		Use data form		
16	-					
17	Print Database	Ordctrl.xdm!Print_it		Print off database		
18	-					
19	Save and Exit	Ordctrl.xdm!Save_Quit		Save database & quit Excel		
20	-					
21	Excel Menus	Ordctrl.xdm!Excel.Menu		Return to Excel menus		
22						
23						
24						
25						
26						
27						
28						

Figure 6.17

Narrow column O to about 1.00 as shown.

2. As a guide enter the heading of the columns in italics as shown. (these headings are not required for the menu table to work)
Column M contains the name of the menu table – Orders – plus the names of the 4 menu options.

Enter the menu name in cell M13 and the menu options in cells M14 to M21 as shown.
The single dash in a cell causes a dividing line to be placed between menu options.

3. In column N enter the names of the macros called by each menu option, as shown in Fig 6.17.
Column O, the middle column of the table is left blank.
Enter the status bar messages in column P as shown. These messages will appear in the Status Bar at the bottom of the screen when a menu option is displayed.
Column Q allows you to provide custom help text, we will not use it in this application.

4. We now need to write two short macros, one to call up the custom menu, and the other to restore the standard Excel menu bar.
Type in the Show_Menu macro in cells P1 – P5 – see Figure 6.18.

	O	P	Q	
1		Show_Menu		
2		=ADD.BAR()	creates a bar	
3		=ADD.MENU(P2,M13:Q19)	adds menu to bar	
4		=SHOW.BAR(P2)	shows bar menu	
5		=RETURN()		
6				
7		Excel_Menu (m)		
8		=SHOW.BAR(1)	restore excel menus	
9		=RETURN()		

Figure 6.18

The =ADD.BAR() function creates a new menu bar, the =SHOW.BAR() function displays it, and the =ADD.MENU() function creates the menu choices based on the table details given in cell range M12 to Q19 (see Figure 6.17).
The P2 in the formulae refers to cell P2.

5. Now key in the Excel.Menu macro in cells P7 – P9.
It will return the user to the normal Excel menu bar after he has used the custom menu.
The function =SHOW BAR(1) displays full worksheet menus. The other options for this function are:
2   full chart menus
3   File menu only
4   Info menus
5   short worksheet menus
6   short chart menus

These options allow us to control further the menu choices available to the user.

6. If you key in a macro, as you have just done, rather than record it, you must define it as a macro.
    Select the macro name Show_Menu in cell P1. Open the Formula menu and select Define Name.
    Type in the macro name in the Name box if necessary. Click the Command button.
    Type the letter l in the 'Ctrl+' box, then click OK.

7. Repeat these operations for the Excel.Menu macro.
    Assign it the letter m.

Activity 13. Testing the Application

> We have now created most of the purchase order application and the custom menu; go to the worksheet ORDENTER and test the application as follows:

1. Press Ctrl-l. The normal Excel menu bar disappears, to be replaced by the custom menu Orders.
    Open it and you will see the 4 options that you have created.
    Keep the mouse button pressed down; as you select each option a different message should appear in the Status Bar.

2. Select the first option – Enter an Order
    The dialogue box should appear; add a new record and return – press the Enter button. The record should be added to the database and you are returned to the worksheet.

3. Select the second option – Edit an Order.
    The Data Form is displayed.
    Check that the new record has been added to the database. Return to the worksheet.

4. Make sure that the printer is turned on.
    Select the third option – Print Database.
    Check that all the records are printed – including the new record.

5. Select the fourth option – Save and Exit.
    Both the worksheet and the macro sheet should be saved and closed and you should exit Excel.
    Start Excel again and re-open the worksheet and the macro sheet. Check that the new record was saved.

6. Now press Ctrl-m. The normal Excel menu bar will re-appear.

7. **Troubleshooting**: If any of the above operations don't work correctly make a full note of the problem.
Don't worry – most applications don't work perfectly the first time!
Return to the macro sheet and check both the syntax of the command functions, plus the spelling of the macro names in column N.
Remember that you can test individual macros a step at a time – see Activity 3, section 2.

Activity 14. Enhancing the Application

By now the Purchase Order system is up and running, but there are still some rough edges:

1. The dialogue box that adds a new record could be improved in several ways:
When the dialogue box appears the previous record is still displayed.
After the record has been added the user should be given the option of adding another.
At the moment the record gets added to the database even if the user selects the Cancel button.

2. The VAT calculations applied to a record take no account of VAT-exempt items.
Remember that on the custom dialogue box there is a button that the user must de-select if VAT is not payable. The VAT calculation needs to test for this.

3. At the moment the user has to remember to open the macro sheet as well as the worksheet.
It would be better if the macro sheet opened automatically whenever the worksheet is opened, and displayed the title screen and custom menu.

4. At the moment the various screens flash by rather distractingly when a macro executes.

5. We will put these problems right in the remaining activities.
Before you start tinkering with the worksheet and macro sheet make back-up copies of them.
This is most easily done when they are open, using the Save as command – see Chapter 1, Activity 13.
Call the copies ORDCTRL.BAK and ORDENTER.BAK

Activity 15. Clearing the Custom Dialogue Box

> This activity creates a macro that clears out the contents of the custom dialogue box so that it is blank when another order is added.
>
> So that we understand the problem let's recap on how the dialogue box is displayed and how it holds the purchase order data:
>
> **a.** The custom dialogue box was designed using the Dialogue Editor – see Activity 4.
> **b.** The specifications were then transferred to the macro sheet – see Activity 5.
> **c.** A macro was written to display the dialogue box – see Activity 5.
> **d.** When this macro is run the user can enter a record – which is then stored in the macro sheet. – see Activity 7.
> **e.** The cells in the macro sheet holding the record are each given a name, so that the data can be transferred to the database in the worksheet ORDENTER – see Activities 7 and 8.
>
> These are the cells that need to be cleared before a new record is added.

1. Activate the macro sheet ORDCTRL.XLM.
   Open the Formula menu and select Goto.
   A dialogue box appears, listing all the named cells and cell ranges.
   Most are macros that we have created, but there are also the cell names created in activity 7 – SUPPLIER, TYPE, etc. – see Figure 6.19.

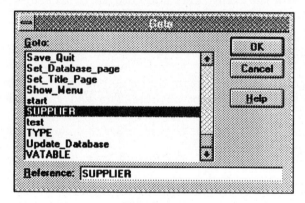

Figure 6.19

   Scroll down to the cell named PRODUCT and click OK – it is selected.

2. Now that we have the hang of this we will record the macro.
   Select cell B75 on the macro sheet – or the first available cell in this column.
   Open the Macro menu and choose Set Recorder.
   Open the Macro menu and select Record; call the macro
   Clear_Dialogue_Box and allocate the letter n.
   You are now recording.

3. Open the Formula menu and select Goto.
    Find the cell name SUPPLIER in the dialogue box.
    Click OK – the cell is selected.
    Open the Edit menu and select Clear.
    A dialogue box appears – select the All option.
    Click OK – the cell contents are cleared, but not the cell name.

4. Now repeat these selection and clearing operations for the following five
    named cells – QUANTITY, PRODUCT, PRICE, DATE and TYPE.
    (You will find it easier to use the Repeat Clear command offered on the Edit
    menu)
    The cell contents should be cleared each time.

5. Stop the Recorder.
    Look at the macro in Figure 6.20.

	A	B
74		
75		Clear_Dialogue_Box (n)
76		**=FORMULA.GOTO("ORDCTRL.XLM!SUPPLIER")**
77		=CLEAR(1)
78		=FORMULA.GOTO("QUANTITY")
79		=CLEAR(1)
80		=FORMULA.GOTO("PRODUCT")
81		=CLEAR(1)
82		=FORMULA.GOTO("PRICE")
83		=CLEAR(1)
84		=FORMULA.GOTO("DATE")
85		=CLEAR(1)
86		=FORMULA.GOTO("TYPE")
87		=CLEAR(1)
88		**=ACTIVATE("ORDENTER.XLS")**
89		=RETURN()

Figure 6.20

It consists of six GOTO and CLEAR functions.
The two lines in bold are amendments you have to make:

a. The first GOTO needs to give an external reference to the macro sheet
    ORDCTRL.XLM, as the Clear_Dialogue_Box macro will be called from
    the worksheet ORDENTER
    The first GOTO will then go to the cell SUPPLIER on the macro sheet
    and all subsequent GOTO's will work.

b. After the macro sheet cells are cleared, the ACTIVATE function ensures
    that the worksheet becomes the active document again.

6. Make these two amendments and then test the macro as follows:

Activate the worksheet and run the Call_Dialogue_box macro. Add a new record, making a note of the data entered.

Open the Macro menu and select Run.

Select the Clear_Dialogue Box macro and press the Step button.

Use the Step Into button to step through the macro, making sure that,

☐ The ORDCTRL macro sheet is activated

☐ Each dialogue box entry is cleared

☐ The worksheet is activated again.

Activity 16. User Choice – Conditions and Loops

A macro can be set up to:

a. prompt the user for a response, e.g. yes or no.

b. Respond to user choice using IF functions – the macro can then branch, i.e. take alternative routes, depending on the choice.

c. Keep repeating until the a certain condition is met. (looping or iteration). At the moment the macro operates once and ends.

We need to modify the macro Update_Database in the above three ways so that the user is prompted to add another record. A 'y' response will keep running the macro until an 'n' is input.

1. At the moment Update_Database merely calls two other macros, Call_Dialogue_Box and Add_Order – see Activity 9, section 6.

2. Find the Update_Database macro on the macro sheet and amend it as shown in Figure 6.21.

	A	B	C
92			
93			
94	cell names	Update_Database (x)	Comments
95	start →	=RUN(ORDCTRL.XLM!Format_Sheet)	Display title screen
96		=RUN(ORDCTRL.XLM!Call_Dialogue_Box)	add new record
97		=IF(ISTEXT(SUPPLIER))	if supplier field completed
98		=RUN(ORDCTRL.XLM!Restore_Screen)	restore standard screen
99		=RUN(ORDCTRL.XLM!Disp_Database)	Display database screen
100		= RUN(ORDCTRL.XLM!Add_Order)	Add order to database
101		=END.IF()	
102		=RUN(ORDCTRL.XLM!Clear_Dialogue_Box)	remove previous record
103	choice →	=INPUT("Add Another Order y/n",2,"Add an Order")	prompt user
104		=IF(choice="y",GOTO(start))	if user types y do again
105		=RUN(ORDCTRL.XLM!Format_Sheet)	if not Display title screen...
106		=RETURN()	.....then finish

Figure 6.21

The gridlines have been set off for readability as the functions are fairly complex.
You will need to be especially careful with the syntax of the brackets, spaces and commas.
Hint. A good check is to enter each function in lower case; if Excel accepts the syntax it will convert the function to upper case. Otherwise it will remain lower case.
Notice also the full comments in column C and the use of column A for cell names. The more sophisticated the application the more complex the macros become; anything that helps readability also helps understanding and future maintenance.

3. Now select the cell containing the first function in the macro; in Figure 6.21 it is cell B95.
   Using the Formula-Define Name command, name this cell Start.
   Similarly name the cell containing the INPUT function Choice – in Figure 6.21 it is cell B103.
   Hint. If you change the position of a named cell, e.g. by inserting or deleting other cells in column B, then the name will no longer apply to this cell; amend the name reference in this situation.

157

4. The INPUT function has the syntax: INPUT(prompt,type[,title,default,x,y])
The INPUT function displays a simple user dialogue box on screen; in this case the prompt is 'Add Another Order y/n' and the title of the box is 'Add an Order' – see cell B103.
Title,default x and y are all optional as indicated by the square brackets – the square brackets themselves are not typed.
Default means the suggested response – in this case we could have a y or an n appear in the dialogue box by default.
x and y are screen coordinates allowing you to position the dialogue box.
Type is the type of information the user can enter – in this case text; possible values are:

0	Formula
1	Number
2	Text
4	Logical
8	Reference
16	Error
64	Array

5. **Conditions and Branching**. There are two IF functions in the macro, testing for different conditions.
The second IF function in cell B104 has the syntax:
IF(condition,true response[,false response])
The condition tested is choice='y', where 'Choice' is the name of the cell receiving the input.
The GOTO function goes back or loops to the cell named 'Start', which starts the Call_Dialogue_Box macro again.
The false response test is optional; if the user enters anything else than a 'y' response then the macro will not run again.

6. The second IF .... END.IF function is more complex and occupies cell range B97 to B101. It prevents a blank record being added to the database using the function ISTEXT.
If there is some text in the cell named SUPPLIER this means that the user must have entered something in the dialogue box – so the record can be added to the data base.
The appropriate macros are run in cells B98 – B100.
If the ISTEXT function finds the cell SUPPLIER empty then the user has clicked the Cancel button on the dialogue box.
In this case the IF condition is false, and the macro continues from the first function after END.IF.
Read the comments in column C carefully to ensure you understand before making the following tests.

7. Activate the worksheet ORDENTER and run the macro Update_Database.
    Enter a new record and click the Enter button.
    The record should be added to the database – you will see this happening.
    The response box appears – 'Add Another Order y/n'
    Key in y and click OK.
    The custom dialogue box re-appears; it should be blank apart from the VAT-able? button which is checked by default.
    Click the Cancel button.
    The ISTEXT function detects the Supplier box is empty this time the database is not updated.
    The response box re-appears, this time key in an n.
    The macro should end.

8. Run the macro again – the blank dialogue box should re– appear.
    Leave the dialogue box empty but click the Enter button. No record should be added.
    When the response box is presented leave it blank but click OK. The macro will end.

9. If you are still unsure about the operation of the macro then step through it a line at a time. This testing may seem tedious but it is the only way to ensure that all conditions are fully covered – especially user errors.

10. Now activate the worksheet ORDENTER and select cell R22 which holds the VAT formula =O22*P22*0.175 – see Activity 8, section 8.

11. Clearly this formula should only operate if the item purchased is eligible for VAT.
    Select cell R22 and amend the formula to:
    =IF(ORDCTRL.XLM!VATABLE=TRUE,O22*P22*0.175,0)
    The syntax of this IF function is similar to the previous ones; it means 'if the value of the cell VATABLE on the macro sheet ORDCTRL is set to TRUE, then let the cell equal cell O22 multiplied by P22 multiplied by 0.175, otherwise let it equal 0'.

12. Let's test it now.
    Press Ctrl-x to run the macro. The dialogue box appears. When entering a record click the VAT-able? button to deselect it.
    A second dialogue box appears, offering the choice to 'Add Another Order y/n' Enter a n.

13. Now check the database that,

    a. The new record has been added,

    b. VAT has not been calculated,

Activity 17. Consolidation

To improve the purchase order application still further make the following final changes:

1. Create an auto_open macro to ensure that the macro sheet ORDCTRL is opened automatically every time the worksheet ORDENTER is opened
    Hint. See Chapter 5, Activity 6.

2. To stop the screen flashing during macro execution insert the =ECHO(FALSE) function at the start of the appropriate macros. It will also stop the screen positions being updated during macro execution.
    Use the ECHO(TRUE) function to set it back on.

3. Ensure that the user always returns to the title screen after using one of the custom menu options.
    Hint. Look at the Update_Database macro – Figure 6.21 – where this has already been implemented.

Summary of Commands and Functions

Notes: Menu commands show the menu name first, followed by the command to choose from the menu, e.g. Edit-Clear means open the Edit menu and select the Clear command.

Commands

Edit-Paste Special	Paste certain features of copied cells e.g. formulae, contents, values only.
Formula-Define Name	name selected cell/cell range/ macro.
Formula-Goto	Select cell by name or reference
Formula-Select Special	Select cells by certain criteria, e.g. contents, range.
Options-Display	Turn on/off features of current window e.g. gridlines, row and column headings.
Options-Workspace	Alter settings for whole session e.g. Status, Scroll and Formula bars

Dialogue Editor Commands

Edit_Copy	Copy selected items in dialogue box
Edit-Info	Edit,move or delete item
Edit-Select Dialogue	Select all items
Item-[various]	Add text, box, button etc. to dialogue box

Functions

Functions require you to supply information for their operations. These are called arguments.
e.g SUM(range) requires the argument cell range to be added.
Arguments must be enclosed in brackets.
Optional arguments are shown in the lists that follow in square brackets – [].
These brackets are for your guidance only and should **not** be typed.
Function arguments are separated by commas.
The commas **must** be typed.

Note: Only the functions that need to be keyed into the macro sheet rather than recorded are given here.

=ACTIVATE(worksheet_name)
Makes named worksheet the current worksheet.

=ADD.BAR([bar_number])
Creates a new menu bar. Options are:
1   full menus
2   full chart menus
3   no menus (except File)
4   Info menu bar
5   short menus
6   short chart menus

=ADD.MENU([bar_number])
Adds a menu to a custom bar previously created by ADD.BAR.
See above for bar numbers.

=DIALOG.BOX(cell_range)
Displays dialogue box given in the specified range on the macro sheet.

=ECHO(FALSE)
Stops the screen flashing/being updated during macro execution.

=ECHO(TRUE)
reverses the =ECHO(FALSE) function

=FILE.CLOSE(document_name)
Closes named worksheet, macro sheet, chart etc.

=FORMULA.GOTO([worksheet_name!]cell_reference/name)
Selects the specified cell.

=GOTO(cell_reference/name)
continues macro at specified cell – used for simple conditional branching or looping.

=IF(condition,true response[,false response])
Tests for condition being true or false.

=IF(condition)
(functions)
[=ELSE()]
(alternative functions)
=END.IF()
Structured conditional functions – If a condition is true then certain functions follow.
If they are not true then optionally an alternative set of functions may be given after the =ELSE() function.
If neither condition applies then the whole IF is bypassed.
An =END.IF()must end the structured IF construct.

=INPUT(prompt,type[,title,default,x,y])
Displays a simple user dialogue box on screen.
A box title can be given and a default suggested response.
x and y screen coordinates allow you to position the dialogue box.
Types of information the user can be required to enter are;

0   Formula
1   Number
2   Text
4   Logical
8   Reference
16   Error
64   Array

=ISTEXT(cell_reference)
checks if cell contents are text; related IS functions are =ISBLANK(), ISNON-TEXT, ISERROR(), ISNUMBER()

=QUIT()
Closes all documents (prompting to save) and exits Excel.

=RETURN()
Ends the current macro.

=RUN([worksheet_name!]macro_name)
Runs named macro.

=SHOW.BAR([bar_number])
Displays a custom menu bar previously defined by =ADD.BAR and =ADD.MENU(). See ADD.BAR for list of bar numbers.

Appendices – Solutions to selected consolidation activities

You are referred, from the text, to these appendices to check your answers in certain consolidation activities.

Appendix 1

INCOME	Week 6	Week 7	Week 8	Week 9	Week 10
Opening Bals.	495.00	365.00	235.00	105.00	-25.00
grant					
loan					
parents					
Total Income	495.00	365.00	235.00	105.00	-25.00
EXPENDITURE					
accommodation	60.00	60.00	60.00	60.00	60.00
food & Travel	35.00	35.00	35.00	35.00	35.00
books	15.00	15.00	15.00	15.00	15.00
other	20.00	20.00	20.00	20.00	20.00
Total Expenditure	130.00	130.00	130.00	130.00	130.00
CLOSING BALS.	365.00	235.00	105.00	-25.00	-155.00

Appendix 2

	A	F	G	H	I	J	K
1							
2							
3	INCOME	Week 5	Week 6	Week 7	Week 8	Week 9	Week 10
4	Opening Bals.	615.00	480.00	365.00	270.00	205.00	110.00
5	grant						
6	loan						
7	Part-time Job			20.00	20.00	20.00	20.00
8	parents				30.00		
9	Total Income	615.00	480.00	385.00	320.00	225.00	130.00
10							
11	EXPENDITURE						
12	accommodation	65.00	65.00	65.00	65.00	65.00	65.00
13	food & Travel	35.00	30.00	30.00	30.00	30.00	30.00
14	books	15.00					
15	other	20.00	20.00	20.00	20.00	20.00	30.00
16	Total Expenditure	135.00	115.00	115.00	115.00	115.00	125.00
17							
18	CLOSING BALS.	480.00	365.00	270.00	205.00	110.00	5.00

Appendix 3

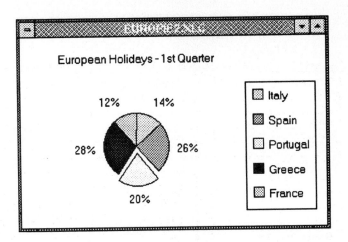

Appendix 4

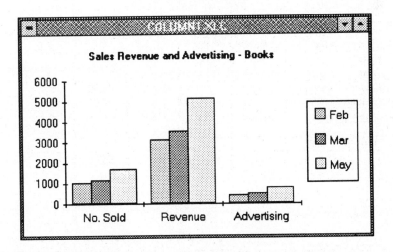

Appendix 5

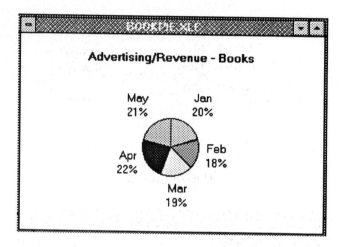

Appendix 6

	A	B	C	D	E
1	Order No.	Order Date	Co. Ref	Co. Name	Value
2	14001	8-Mar	2413	Patel Industries	1466.00
3	14007	9-Mar	1453	Wilson Garages	2654.00
4	14000	10-Mar	1453	Wilson Garages	3200.44
5	14004	10-Mar	2413	Patel Industries	567.00
6	14006	10-Mar	2375	Patel Kitchens	55.44
7	14003	11-Mar	1289	Marsden Products	4456.00
8	14005	11-Mar	955	Tilley Transport	1678.09
9	14002	11-Mar	1453	Wilson Garages	98.76
10	14009	12-Mar	1289	Marsden Products	1652.54
11	14008	12-Mar	2245	Goldfield Stables	123.85

Appendix 7

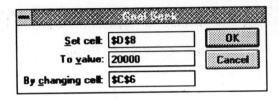

Appendix 8

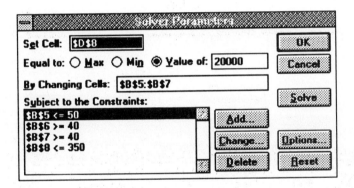

Index

dBase for Business Students – Incorporating III and IV

J Muir

An Active-Learning Approach

ISBN: **1 873981 16 3** • Date: **1992** • Edition: **1st**
Extent: **192 pp** • Size: **245 x 190 mm**

Courses on which this book is known to be used
BA Business Studies; BTEC National and Higher National Business and Finance, and Computing; BSc Computing; IIM; BEngineering; MBA

This book is aimed at students on a wide variety of business courses who need to know how to use dBase III and IV (including dBase IV Version 1.5). The learning material in this book requires minimal, if any, input by lecturers and can be recommended for student self-instruction. It makes no assumptions about business or computing knowledge, but teaches dBase techniques and their business applications in simple terms.

All students can successfully use this book – from those needing only an introduction to those needing advanced programming skills. It covers the essentials of dBase at each level. The text covers all three modes of dBase – menu-driven, command driven, and programming. dBase features are progressively introduced in the context of practical business activities.

Note: A copyright free 3 $\frac{1}{2}$" (720K) disk is provided free of charge to lecturers adopting the book as a course text. It includes all the programs, databases, etc used in the book.

Contents:

Introduction – Databases in Business • Using the Assist and Control Centre • Creating and Searching a Database • Views and Queries – Retrieving Selected Records • Modifying the Database Structure • Adding and Deleting Records • Indexing and Sorting • Producing Printed Reports • Designing Data Entry Screens • Checking User Input • The Applications Generator • Using the Dot Prompt to Create and Search a Database • Dot Prompt Commands • Creating and Running a Program • Program Debugging • Programming Using Screens • Decisions and Conditions – IF and DO CASE Commands • Looping or Iteration – DO WHILE...ENDDO • Locating Duplicate Records • Using Multiple Databases – Updating and Joining • Passing Parameters Between Programs • Conclusion – Bringing It All Together.

Review Comments:

'A first class approach to any learning process involving computers.' 'Practical approach helps make basic lessons lead somewhere.' 'Ideal book for all students, from beginners to revision/reference.' 'I like the guided/independent activity approach, the way the objectives of each section are clearly stated.' 'Useful to have co-ordinated exercises based around the course study.' **– Lecturers**

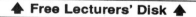

Free Lecturers' Disk

Paradox 4.0 for Students   *PM Heathcote*

An Active-Learning Approach

ISBN: **1 85805 042 1** • Date: **April 1993** • Edition: **1st**
Extent: **224 pp** • Size: **245 x 190 mm**

This book is aimed at any student of business or computing who needs to learn the basics of Borland's Paradox database (Version 4.0), and will enable the student to set up and use any Paradox database. A student who has followed through the various stages of building the case study application (see below) will have a good overview of the package's capabilities and be able to make effective use of Borland's Paradox User Guide for very advanced features not covered in the book.

The book introduces the concept of the database through the use of a case study of a newsagent who wishes to keep details of newspaper deliveries and customer accounts.

In Part 1 of the book, one table containing customer details is used in examples, and the student builds up and queries a second table holding details of newspapers through exercises at the end of chapters.

In Part 2 of the book, the student is shown how to link these two tables through the use of a third table and design more complex data entry and report forms, make more complex queries and perform updates. Simple scripts are introduced.

Part 3 covers the basics of the Application Workshop, using the 'building blocks' (tables, forms, reports, etc) created in the first two Parts of the book, to build a complete menu-driven application.

The student learns through a series of sessions, which tell him or her exactly what steps to follow, and the keystrokes to make, to build and use a database. These steps are then reinforced through the use of exercises at the end of most sessions.

A Lecturers' Supplement is available in the form of 2 disks which contains the completed sample application together with the test data used in the book. The disk also contains, in a series of different directories, the state of the application as it should be at various key points, so that students who have forgotten, mislaid or corrupted their disks can be brought up to date without having to repeat stages already covered.

Contents:

Part 1 – Building and Using Unrelated Tables

The Basics • Creating a Table • Adding Data • Managing the Desktop • Editing • Data Entry Forms • Making Queries • Sorting • Tabular Reports • Free-form Reports • Graphs • Password Protection • File Management.

Part 2 – Building a Relational Database

Relating Tables in a Database • Querying Multiple Tables • Advanced Report Techniques • Forms Using Multiple Tables • Automatic Updating • Scripts • Introduction to PAL Programming.

Part 3 – The Application Workshop

Planning the Application • Creating the Menu Bar • Defining Action Objects • Testing and Modifying.

♠ Free Lecturers' Disk ♠

MS Works

D Weale

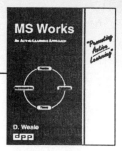

ISBN: **1 873981 30 9** • Date: **1992** • Edition: **1st**
Extent: **144 pp** • Size: **245 x 190 mm**

Courses on which this book is known to be used
BTEC First and National, A Level Computing, and the many courses requiring a basic knowledge of spreadsheets, databases and word processing via MS Works.

The aim of the book is to provide a 'user friendly' guide for students being introduced to spreadsheets, databases and word processing via MS Works.

It is very much a 'learning by doing' guide – requiring very little (if any) input from the lecturer, enabling students to learn and practice the commands and techniques using examples to which they can relate, ie business ones. A series of sessions, each self-contained, takes students step by step to a level at which they can happily use the program manual to master finer details.

Contents:

Loading Works • Works on-line help • How to use a mouse with Works • The Works tutorial • Sorting out problems • Keyboard characters • **Word Processing** Getting started • Formatting • Tabs and tables • Layout • Spelling and searching • Borders and fonts • Consolidation • **Spreadsheets and charts** • Spreadsheets • Formulae • Layout and format • Editing and sorting • Graphs and charts • Graphs and formulae • Consolidation • **Databases** Databases • Searching • Reports • **Using MS Works in an integrated way** • **Appendices** Suggestions on layout • Summary of commands • File management • Configuring the system.

Review Comments:

'Excellent for self-study and hands on experience using MS Works.' 'A first class training course that leads to a high degree of operational efficiency.' 'Excellent value for money.' 'Good presentation. Detailed step-by-step instruction.'
– Lecturers

♠ Free Lecturers' Disk ♠

Word for Windows
An Active-Learning Approach

J Rowley
S Coles

ISBN: **1 85805 047 2** • Date: **September 1993** • Edition: **1st**
Extent: **200 pp (approx)** • Size: **245 x 190 mm**

This book is aimed primarily at students on a wide variety of business studies courses (including BTEC National, BTEC Higher, and undergraduate courses in accountancy, computing and information systems), but is equally applicable to many other courses where students need to be able to word process their assignments or projects.

The book introduces the student to the basics of word processing through a series of applications-oriented exercises. A series of self-contained sessions takes the student through the production of various types of document, and gradually introduces the student to the features and functions of the word processing package.

As each new function is introduced, the book explains why the function is useful and how to use it.

The learning material requires little, if any, input by the lecturer and can therefore be used in programmes based on independent learning. Students learn by practising the commands and techniques to produce specific types of document.

Contents:

Letter and Memos: Basics; Advertisements and Posters; Formatting Text; Improving your Documents; Tables and Questionnaires; Tabulation; Report and Assignments; Large Documents; Charts in Documents; Images in Documents; Newsletters; Columns; Special Applications • Appendix 1 – Basic Windows Operations • Appendix 2 – Buttons on the Default Toolbar • Appendix 3 – Customising Word.

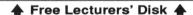 **Free Lecturers' Disk**

SuperCalc 5
An Active-Learning Approach

PH Bassett

ISBN: **1 85805 048 0** • Date: **August 1993** • Edition: **1st**
Extent: **200 pp (approx)** • Size: **245 x 190 mm**

This book is designed with two principal objectives in mind: firstly, that the user should be able to develop skills in using the various SuperCalc commands and formulae; secondly, that the user should develop an awareness of the possible applications that SuperCalc can be used for.

The book is essentially targeted at Computing and Business Studies students. However, as users get to grips with the commands they should be able to develop applications within other functional areas as well.

Designed as a teach-yourself guide to the SuperCalc spreadsheet program, the book is divided into individual lessons, each covering some of the commands and options available when using SuperCalc. Sample exercises are included at the end of each lesson so that the user can practise the command taught in that lesson. Where applicable, answers to these exercises can be found at the end of the book.

Note: as far as the author is aware, the book can be used on all 'bug free' versions of SuperCalc 5.

Contents:

The Basics of SuperCalc – Common SuperCalc Commands – Improving Sales Graphs – Budgets – Break Even Analysis – Stock Control – Payroll – Advanced Payroll – Databases – Statistics and Advanced Graphics – Financial Applications – Job Costing – Macros and Audit Commands – Summary of Commands and Functions

♠ **Free Lecturers' Disk** ♠

Spreadsheets for Business Students
An Active-Learning Approach

C West

ISBN: **1 873981 16 3** • Date: **1991** • Edition: **1st**
Extent: **192 pp** • Size: **245 x 190 mm**

Courses on which this book is known to be used
BTEC National Higher National Business and Finance, and Computing; BA Business Studies; ACCA; AAT; IPM; DMS; CLAIT III; NEBSM

The aim of this book is to provide a 'user friendly' guide for students on the innumerable courses where acquaintance with the basics of spreadsheets is required.

It is very much a 'learning by doing' guide – requiring very little (if any) input by the lecturer and can be used on any machine/system with Lotus 1-2-3 version 2.0 (or above) or compatible spreadsheets such as VP-Planner and As-Easy-As.

All examples have a business emphasis and students progressively gain confidence in the basics of:

❏ constructing spreadsheet models

❏ saving and retrieving files

❏ graphics

❏ printing spreadsheets and graphs

❏ using a spreadsheet as a data base

❏ creating and using simple macros.

The lecturers' supplement is a copyright-free $5\frac{1}{4}$" (360K) PC-compatible disk, incorporating files in .WKS format for the models in the book, for checking students' activities.

Contents:

Models include:

VAT Calculations • Cash Flow Forecast • Integrated Cash Flow Forecast/ Profit & Loss Account/Balance Sheet • Accounting Ratios • Cost Behaviour • Cost Allocation and Apportionment • Cost-Volume-Profit Analysis.

Each session contains:

Objectives • Active Learning • Summary • Activities • Objective (Multi-choice) Test.

Review Comments:

*'I like the worksheet approach enabling students to work at their own pace.' 'A wonderful time saver – congratulations.' 'Ideal for new modularised units – all activity based.' 'Tried it on 2 lecturers first – they found it easy, so able now to recommend it to students!' 'Good to use in open learning workshop.' 'Excellent in every way – a book like this, at its current price, has been wanted for years!' 'Student friendly – makes spreadsheet manuals obsolete, very competitive.' – **Lecturers***

'A good introduction to using a spreadsheet package.' **"Company Accountant"**

⬥ Free Lecturers' Disk ⬥

Spreadsheets for Accountancy Students
An Active-Learning Approach

C West

ISBN: **1 873981 31 7** • Date: **1992** • Edition: **1st**
Extent: **368 pp** • Size: **245 x 190 mm**

Courses on which this book is known to be used
BA Business Studies/Accounting; ACCA; AAT; CIMA; BTEC HND; DMS; MBA. All professional accountancy courses and accountancy degree courses, and accounting options on business courses.

The aim of the book is to provide a 'user friendly' guide for accountancy students. It is very much a 'learning by doing' guide – requiring very little (if any) input by the lecturer and can be used on any machine/system with Lotus 1-2-3 version 2.0 (or above) or compatible spreadsheets such as VP-Planner and As-Easy-As.

The book is in two parts:

Part A: Apart from minor amendments, this Part is the complete content of *Spreadsheets for Business Students* as accountancy students, starting from scratch, need a foundation of these more basic techniques before concentrating on those aspects **specific** to accountants.

Part B: This consists of a series of 21 models, some interrelated, covering **financial accounting**, **management accounting**, and **financial management**. Basic skills will be learned through applying spreadsheet principles to solve accountancy problems.

The lecturers' supplement is a copyright-free $3\frac{1}{2}$" (720K) PC-compatible disk, incorporating files mainly in .WKS format for the models in the book, for checking students' activities.

Contents:

Part A – *Models include:*
VAT Calculations • Cash Flow Forecast • Integrated Cash Flow Forecast/ Profit & Loss Account/Balance Sheet • Accounting Ratios • Cost Behaviour • Cost Allocation and Apportionment • Cost-Volume-Profit Analysis.

Each session contains:
Objectives • Active Learning • Summary • Activities • Objective (Multi-choice) Test.

Part B – A wide range of Financial Accounting, Management Accounting and Financial Management Models

Each session contains:
Objectives • Active Learning • Problem • Model Solution: Creation and Explanation • Activity.

Review Comments:

'Excellent value for money ... simply has no serious competitors.' 'User friendly, logical progression and good value for money.' 'Well structured and comprehensive course text.' 'An excellent text that will lead to both greater appreciation of accounting methodology, and improved computer skills.' 'A well written text, covering topics precisely ... good value.' – **Lecturers**

⬥ **Free Lecturers' Disk** ⬥

Tackling Computer Projects

PM Heathcote

ISBN: **1 85805 002 2** • Date: **1992** • Edition: **1st**
Extent: **240 pp** • Size: **275 x 215 mm**

Courses on which this book is known to be used
A Level Computing, BTEC National and Higher National Computing

---

Contents:

Part 1: Choosing a Project. Analysis. Design. Using a Package. Pascal Techniques. Testing. The Report

Part 2: Specimen Project 1 – Gilbert and Sullivan Society Patrons List Analysis. Design. Testing. System Maintenance. User Manual. Appraisal.

Part 3: Specimen Project 2 – Short Course Database Analysis. Design. Testing. System Maintenance. Appraisal. User Manual. Appendices: Paradox Script. Test Runs.

Appendices: Turbo Pascal Editing Keys and Blank Forms

The aim of this book is to provide students with a comprehensive and practical guide on how to tackle a computing project for an Advanced Level or BTEC National computing course, using either a programming language or a software package. It will also be useful to students doing a project for a GCSE computing course or a Higher National computing course, since the principles remain the same at any level.

Students very often find it difficult to think of a suitable idea for a computer project, and having come up with an idea, find the analysis and design stages extremely difficult to get started on. This book gives them plenty of ideas for possible projects with advice on what constitutes a suitable project and a complete specimen project of each type (programming and package implementation) together with advice on how each stage (analysis, design, etc) is tackled.

The first project is implemented in Pascal and the accompanying listing is used to illustrate many useful techniques in Turbo Pascal such as pop-up windows and the use of function keys. The second example illustrates how to tackle a project using a software package instead of a suite of programs. Borland's Paradox database (Version 3.5) has been used, but the actual package is not of any significance here as the emphasis is on how to analyse, design, test and document the system.

Review Comments:

'It is ideal for our BTEC students to help them to tackle programming projects in a realistic and down-to-earth way, encouraging good practice – very readable too!' 'It tackles areas other texts ignore eg testing approaches and creation of a user manual, etc'. 'Well thought out and thorough advice for students on their project work for A Level – in fact for any level later too!' 'This is just the book required for students. It fills a gap in the market since other texts devote at most a single chapter to this 'grey area'. 'It is an excellent aid and should sell very well.'

– Lecturers

▲ **Free Lecturers' Supplement**   **Free Lecturers' Supplement** ▲

— 🍏 —

You like this book? Perhaps we have another to help you with your studies:

Title	Author	Price
☐ Accounting & Finance for Business Students	Bendrey et al	£10.95
☐ Advanced Level Accounting	Randall	£11.95
☐ Advanced Level Biology Practical	Hawkes/Eldridge	£8.95
☐ Advanced Level Business Studies	Danks	£9.95
☐ Advanced Level Maths	Solomon	£9.95
☐ Advanced Level Maths Revision Course	Solomon	£4.95
☐ Auditing	Millichamp	£9.95
☐ BASIC Programming	Holmes	£7.95
☐ Business Accounting I Active Learning	Randall	£12.95
☐ Business Maths & Statistics	Francis	£9.95
☐ Business Law	Abbott/Pendlebury	£10.95
☐ Company Law	Abbott	£9.95
☐ Computer Science	French	£11.95
☐ Computer Studies	French	£7.95
☐ Computing Active Learning	Heathcote	£9.95
☐ Convert to C & C++	Holmes	£9.95
☐ Cost & Management Accounting Active Learning	Lucey	£9.95
☐ Costing	Lucey	£10.95
☐ Data Processing	French	£8.95
☐ dBase for Business Students	Muir	£5.95
☐ Discovering Marketing Active Learning	Stokes	£9.95
☐ Discovering the World of Business	Hillas	£8.95
☐ Easy Guide to Casio Scientific Calculator	Payne	£2.00
☐ Economics for Professional & Business Students	Powell	£9.95
☐ Elements of Marketing	Morden	£11.95
☐ English for Business	Chilver	£6.95
☐ Finance for Non-Financial Managers	Millichamp	£9.95
☐ Financial Accounting Study Text	Jennings	£11.95
☐ Financial Accounting Solutions Manual	Jennings	£8.95
☐ Financial Management	Brockington	£9.95
☐ Financial Record Keeping	Lee/Jarvis	£8.95
☐ First Course in Business Maths & Statistics	Rowe	£4.95
☐ First Course in Business Studies	Danks	£6.95
☐ First Course in Cost & Management Accounting	Lucey	£6.95
☐ First Course in Marketing	Jefkins	£6.95
☐ First Course in Statistics	Booth	£5.95
☐ First Level Management Active Learning	Lang	£8.95
☐ Foundation Accounting	Millichamp	£9.95
☐ GCSE English	Tarbitt	£6.50
☐ GCSE French	Kambuts/Wilson	£7.50
☐ GCSE Mathematics	Solomon	£7.95
☐ GCSE Maths Higher Level	Solomon	£7.95
☐ GCSE Maths Practice Papers Higher	McCarthy	£3.95
☐ GCSE Maths Practice Papers Intermediate	McCarthy	£3.95
☐ GCSE Maths Revision Course Higher	McCarthy	£3.95
☐ GCSE Maths Revision Course Intermediate	McCarthy	£3.95
☐ GCSE Modern World History	Snellgrove	£6.50
☐ GCSE Science Quizbook	Freemantle	£2.95
☐ Information Technology Skills & Knowledge	Harris/Hogan	£7.95
☐ Intermediate Accounting	Dyson	£7.95
☐ Introductory Pascal	Holmes	£5.95
☐ Introductory Microprocessors & Microcomputer Technology	Hanley	£7.95

Title	Author	Price
☐ Local Area Networks	Hodson	£6.95
☐ Management Accounting	Lucey	£10.95
☐ Management Information Systems	Lucey	£7.95
☐ Management, Theory & Practice	Cole	£10.95
☐ Maths Attainment Tests Key Stage 1	Burndred	£3.75
☐ Maths Attainment Tests Key Stage 2	Burndred	£3.95
☐ Maths Attainment Tests Key Stage 3	Burndred	£3.95
☐ Maths for Engineering	Clarke	£7.95
☐ Maths Key Stage 4 Vol. 1	Solomon	£6.50
☐ Vol. 2	Solomon	£6.50
☐ Vol. 3	Solomon	£6.50
☐ Modula-2 Programming	Holmes	£11.95
☐ Off to University?	Alger	£4.95
☐ Operating Systems	Ritchie	£9.95
☐ MS Works	Weale	£5.95
☐ Paradox 4.0 for Students Active Learning	Heathcote	£5.95
☐ PASCAL CORE Active Learning	Boyle/Margetts	£9.95
☐ PASCAL Programming	Holmes	£11.95
☐ Personnel Management	Cole	£10.95
☐ Quantitative Methods for Computing Students	Catlow	£9.95
☐ Quantitative Techniques	Lucey	£9.95
☐ Quantitative Approaches to Decision Making	Oakshott	£9.95
☐ Refresher in Basic Maths	Rowe	£4.95
☐ Refresher in French	Francey	£7.95
☐ Science Attainments Tests Key Stage 3	Burndred/Turnbull	£3.95
☐ Small Business Management Active Learning	Stokes	£9.95
☐ Spreadsheets for Accounting Students	West	£8.95
☐ Spreadsheets for Business Students	West	£5.95
☐ Structured Programming In COBOL	Holmes	£11.95
☐ Students Guide to Accounting & Financial Reporting Standards	Black	£6.95
☐ Systems Analysis & Design	Hughes	£9.95
☐ Tackling Computer Projects	Heathcote	£6.95
☐ Taxation	Rowes	£11.95
☐ Taxation Questions & Answers	Deane	£7.95
☐ Understanding Business & Finance	Hussey	£9.95
☐ Understanding Business Statistics	Saunders/Cooper	£9.95
☐ Understanding Computer Systems Architecture	Lacy	£10.95

DP Publications' books are available in most academic bookshops or, if you have difficulty finding what you want, UK customers can order direct from us at the following address:

DP Publications Ltd,
Aldine House, Aldine Place, London W12 8AW

Reference: B521

Add £2 postage and packing for one book, or £3 p&p for two or more books.

Please send me the titles indicated. I enclose a cheque for £_____.

Name _____

Address _____

_____

_____